Sweet & Unique

CUPCAKE TOPPERS

Over
80
CREATIVE FONDANT TUTORIALS, TIPS, and TRICKS

Sweet & Unique
CUPCAKE TOPPERS

LYNLEE NORTH BECKETT

No part of this book may be reproduced in any form whatsoever, whether by graphic, visual, electronic, film, microfilm, tape recording, or any other means, without prior written permission of the publisher, except in the case of brief passages embodied in critical reviews and articles.

The opinions and views expressed herein belong solely to the author and do not necessarily represent the opinions or views of Cedar Fort, Inc. Permission for the use of sources, graphics, and photos is also solely the responsibility of the author.

ISBN 13: 978-1-4621-1366-8

Published by Front Table Books, an imprint of Cedar Fort, Inc.
2373 W. 700 S., Springville, UT 84663
Distributed by Cedar Fort, Inc., www.cedarfort.com

Library of Congress Cataloging-in-Publication Data on file

Cover and page design by Erica Dixon
Cover design © 2014 by Lyle Mortimer
Edited by Casey J. Winters

Printed in the United States of America

10 9 8 7 6 5 4 3 2 1

TO ANABELLE
My sweetest cupcake, with all my love.

CONTENTS

Fondant
CUPCAKE TOPPERS

97

SOUND THE ALARM

101

MAD SCIENCE

105

WORK OF ART

109

SURF'S UP!

115

NOW SHOWING

119

ROCK THE BEAT

123

NOTHING BUT NET

127

TOUCHDOWN

131

TAKE ME OUT
TO THE BALLGAME

135
FORE!

139
JUST FOR KICKS

145
START YOUR ENGINES

149
SNOWBALL PENGUIN

153
BOOKWORM

159
CONGRATS, GRAD!

161
WE GO TOGETHER LIKE
PEAS & CARROTS

165
LOVE BUGS

167
SOMEWHERE
OVER THE RAINBOW

171

HOPPY EASTER

175

SPRING CHICK

177

OLE! CINCO DE MAYO!

181

COULDN'T PICK
A BETTER MUM

183

DAPPER DAD

187

RED, WHITE & BOOM

191

JACK O' LANTERN
COSTUME PARTY

197

GOBBLE 'TIL
YOU WOBBLE

201

DREIDEL, DREIDEL,
DREIDEL

205
SANTA

207
MERRY & BRIGHT
REINDEER

211
SANTA ON VACATION

215
BABY NEW YEAR

219
BEARY SWEET BABY

223
OOH LA LA

227
BINKY BABY

229
SHABBY CHIC
BRIDAL SHOWER

233
GOING TO THE CHAPEL

Preface

What's a party without cake? As famous chef Julia Child once said, "A party without cake is just a meeting." I completely agree and firmly believe that a celebration is simply not complete without this sweet dessert.

While growing up, our family birthdays and commemorations always included themed cakes, intricately decorated by my father with frosting and decorating tips.

As soon as I was old enough, I began to follow in his footsteps as he taught me to utilize the necessary tools to create cakes for life's special occasions. I became more involved in planning our parties, and the entertaining bug was permanently implanted in me!

Though entertaining didn't initially translate into a career, I continued to decorate cakes and plan parties into adulthood and also began my love affair with cupcakes! Cupcakes are the perfect individual-sized treats fit for kids and adults of all ages. I began to appreciate the endless possibilities centered around the decorating and displaying of these petite sweets, along with the facility in serving them to guests. Cupcakes also became ideal gifts for friends and coworkers, and as a simple symbol of gratitude!

Once my daughter, Anabelle, was born, my aptitude for party planning and cupcake decorating became an undeniable passion—I dedicated countless hours to executing her birthday festivities. As her third birthday approached, I hit a creative roadblock and lacked embellishment ideas to match her cowgirl theme. I browsed the Internet for inspiration and saw several adorable horses made out of fondant, a medium that frankly intimidated me despite the urging of my father to attempt working with it.

Top: Me with a birthday cake made by my father. **Bottom left:** Fondant horse cupcake toppers for my daughter's third birthday. **Bottom right:** My daughter, Anabelle, at her western-themed birthday party.

Knowing these horses would be the perfect adornment to Anabelle's cowgirl cupcakes, I decided to face my fears, buy some fondant, and attempt making western-themed toppers. I was instantly hooked and so began my journey into the fondant cupcake topper world and my new career!

As I began selling fondant cupcake toppers and founded Lynlee's Petite Cakes, the demand grew tremendously, as did the request for tutorials by readers, customers, and fans. I started to provide more step-by-step instructions on my website, in party magazines, and in my own publications, and the exciting response inspired me to write this book, a compilation of tutorials for my most popular and unique designs.

When I was just starting out, I decided to make an investment in only the most basic tools that were easily found at my local craft and baking stores. There was a plethora of metal cutters perfect for cookies, but they weren't small enough for the miniature shapes needed for cupcake toppers, which forced me to get creative with the more accessible equipment available for the general public. Over the years, I have accumulated a variety of miniature cutters, but since I know these tools might be more difficult to acquire, the tutorials included in this book utilize basic cutters and tools that anyone can locate in nationwide stores or online.

Throughout the book are instructions complemented with detailed photographs for you to create over eighty fun and creative cupcake toppers for birthdays, holidays, and many more occasions! Varying difficulty levels allow for anyone to take cupcakes to the next level, along with fondant tips and tricks. Whether you are just starting out or are already a fondant aficionado, I hope you will find inspiration to adorn your cupcakes and transform them into showstopping works of art!

Sweet Tips
FOR USING THIS BOOK

Depending on the number of designs, you will find several tutorials for the cupcake toppers included within each collection, along with advice and tips pertaining to each theme. The following are the categories provided to aid you in customizing the cupcakes based on your particular needs.

Difficulty Levels

Each tutorial is given a level of difficulty, graded by the number of cupcakes assigned.

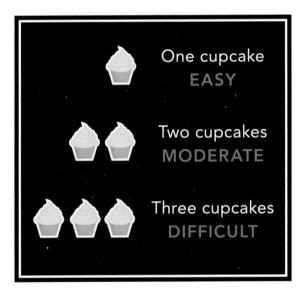

One cupcake
EASY

Two cupcakes
MODERATE

Three cupcakes
DIFFICULT

Don't be hesitant or afraid of the initial ratings! If the design appeals to you but you feel you are not quite ready to attempt it, make sure you look for the "Simplify" category to find recommendations on how to facilitate the steps.

Simplify

With the knowledge that there are so many varying levels of experience, I made sure to include some tips on how to break down the design to make it a little easier but still achieve the overall theme.

Accentuate

Having made cupcake toppers for several years for an abundance of customers and events, I am well aware of the amount of time that is consumed to make each individual design. My work is often recognized as intricate and detailed, which requires many, many hours of labor, especially when creating a large quantity of toppers. The time required to duplicate the embellishments for a great volume of cupcakes is somewhat unrealistic, which is why I included this category to provide simpler ideas to accentuate your presentation. The key is to balance out your elaborate toppers with less complicated ones to, in turn, balance out your schedule!

Personalize

One of the best aspects of making your own fondant cupcake toppers is the ability to match them to your specific theme and personalize them for the guests of honor or the gift receivers. This category will provide you with ideas using certain elements, such as initials or ages, to customize the designs.

Expand

Several of the collections have opportunities to expand the fondant topper assortment with a design found in another tutorial. When you see this category, refer to the noted collection and simply adjust any colors or details when necessary.

Decorate & Display

The fondant cupcake topper designs in this book will undoubtedly be the center of attention, but you can further accentuate them with cupcake and frosting decorations as well as creative displays at parties and celebrations. Refer to this category for suggestions to complete your visual presentation.

Fondant
BASICS

Rolled fondant is likened to a sweet dough, comprised mostly of sugar, water, and corn syrup and most commonly used to decorate cakes and pastries. Similar to clay or play dough, you are able to mold fondant into endless shapes and sizes and create thematic designs—and it is edible! There are many different recipes to make fondant, of which the outcomes can vary in terms of texture, pliability, and firmness. Also, a variety of companies sell premade fondant, which is my personal preference. I primarily work with Satin Ice and Wilton brands, but I've listed additional companies in "Resources & Credits" (p. 239). If you are looking to make your own fondant, feel free to browse through cookbooks and online recipes to give them a try. A popular recipe in the baking world is a variation of a traditional marshmallow fondant by Elizabeth Marek of the Artisan Cake Company. View the recipe at www.artisancakecompany.com /tutorials/lmf-fondant-recipe/.

FONDANT HANDLING AND TEMPERAMENT

Fondant is pliable and can be easy to work with when you are familiar with its temperamental characteristics. When modeling fondant with your hands, it can often get stuck on your fingers, which is why having vegetable shortening on hand is key. Dabbing shortening on your fingers and hands will ensure the fondant doesn't get sticky while you work with it and color it. And since shortening is practically flavorless, its use on fondant won't make a difference in the taste.

You will also need a food-safe mat with a non-stick surface on which to work with your fondant. Most mats specific for fondant or dough will also have grid lines that can be extremely helpful when following tutorials and measurements for precise sizing. My favorites are silicone mats that lie flat on your work surface and are simple to clean.

Along with shortening and a mat, an essential for working with fondant is powdered sugar. You can use a dusting pouch or jar/shaker with small holes in the lid to dust your work surface with powdered sugar, which keeps the fondant from sticking to the mat.

Although fondant is malleable, once it is exposed to air you must work fairly quickly when modeling it; if you let it sit out for several minutes and then attempt to model, cut, or bend it again, you will immediately see it crack, break, or show what bakers often refer to as "elephant skin." Store fondant you are not currently working with in plastic wrap, or inside ziplock bags, in an airtight container. That being said, fondant can take twenty-four to forty-eight hours to dry completely, so when planning out your schedule, make sure you give your cupcake toppers ample time to dry prior to your event. When making three-dimensional figures or shapes that require quite a bit of fondant, I suggest kneading a pinch or two of tylose powder into the fondant to make it stiffer and hold its shape better. When allowing the fondant toppers to dry, I place them on a baking sheet sprinkled with powdered sugar or lined with parchment paper until they are ready to be placed on cupcakes. If you are planning on covering the entire surface of a cupcake with fondant in a dome shape, instead of making the fondant in advance, you must do so at the same time you are frosting your cupcake because the fondant must be pliable to fit over it.

Fondant, especially commercial brands, can last quite a long time. If purchasing it, make sure to check the expiration date on the packaging. The best way to store leftover fondant is to apply a bit of shortening over it and wrap it in plastic wrap. When I know I am going to use the fondant right away, I like to utilize ziplock bags, removing as much air as possible. When storing your finished cupcake toppers, make sure they are in a cool, dry place away from sunlight to avoid discoloration. Certain colors, such as pink and purple, will fade easily when exposed to light, so I will often cover the toppers loosely with aluminum foil to preserve the initial colors. Do not store your fondant cupcake toppers in the refrigerator or freezer because the condensation that will occur when they are taken out can ruin your designs. Storing them in an airtight container can preserve the fondant, but be aware that this can soften the fondant

considerably and it won't hold its original shape.

Attaching your fondant toppers to cupcakes is simple, but your timing is important. All you need to adhere your topper to the cupcake is a bit of frosting, but be aware that the moisture from the icing can seep into the fondant and soften it. I will typically add my cupcake toppers the day of the event, not long before I am setting them out or giving them as a gift. Hot weather and humidity are not friends of fondant! Much like myself, exposure to these extreme conditions will cause the fondant to melt and lose its shape.

As I mentioned at the beginning of this section, fondant can be temperamental, but knowing how it reacts to different ingredients and environments will facilitate its preparation and handling. Just like most things in life, practice makes perfect! Okay, well, maybe not perfect, but practice will definitely help immensely in making you feel comfortable with fondant.

Fondant
COLORING & PAINTING

If you are purchasing fondant, many brands offer it already colored, but it can be costly to acquire every single color, and it still might not be your desired shade. I usually buy white fondant as well fondant in the hard-to-tint colors, namely black and red. Then I invest in gel pastes to color my white fondant. Various websites provide tips for mixing colors to achieve the correct hues as well as how to mix and pair colors for an optimal palette. I have listed a few in "Resources & Credits" (p. 240).

The best way to color fondant is to utilize gel pastes since liquid food coloring adds too much moisture to the fondant and changes its consistency, making it sticky and difficult to model. To avoid walking around with colored hands, use food-safe gloves when tinting fondant. Some gel pastes come in a squeeze bottle, which I pour first into a bowl or cup and then add to the fondant because I have more control over the amount used.

To begin coloring, simply dip a toothpick in the gel paste color desired and apply it to your fondant. Always start off with a small amount of the gel paste because you can always add more color if necessary. Then knead the fondant together with your hands until the color is evenly spread throughout. If mixing colors, you don't have to mix the gels together beforehand. Instead, apply them directly to the fondant before kneading. Add shortening intermittently when necessary. And remember: it's much simpler to make a little more fondant than you need than to not have enough and have to match your original color.

Most tutorials in this book require simple colorations and can be achieved by fluctuating the amount of easy-to-find gel pastes added to the fondant. For example, tan, light brown, brown, and dark brown are used in several collections, but all colors can be achieved by applying brown gel paste to white fondant with an ascending amount of paste. In the table below are some additional colors requiring a mix of two or more paste colors, along with ratios to achieve the comparable shade.

Tan	4 white + 1 brown
Sand	4 ivory + 1 white
Light Gray	4 white +1 black
Maroon	6 red + 1 black
Turquoise	3 blue + 1 yellow
Teal	4 white + 3 blue + 1 green
Mustard Yellow	4 yellow + 1 brown
Burnt Orange	4 orange + 1 brown
Light Peach	1 pink + 2 yellow + 4 white

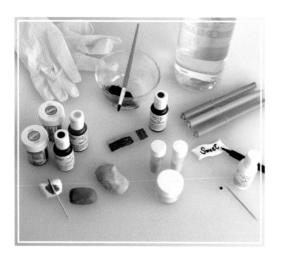

A few tutorials call for a "desired skin color," which can be achieved with variations of ivory, copper, or brown. For further details and online links regarding mixing colors, please reference the color mixing and design section in "Resources & Credits" (p. 240).

If you are trying to achieve a marbled look, color two pieces of fondant separately and then combine them by twisting together, but avoid blending them completely.

Painting fondant is another way to add color and dimension to your designs. Depending on the effect you are trying to achieve, you can use pure colored gel paste or mix it with a bit of water for a simple additive coat, such as for a wood-grain or a vintage look. You can also use shimmer dusts, either brushed on directly to the fondant for glitter and shine or mixed with a clear alcohol, such as vodka, since the alcohol will evaporate and you can paint the fondant safely. Edible-ink markers are also a great way to add details and write on your toppers but are best used when the fondant is completely dry.

One of my favorite aspects of fondant figures is what I refer to as eye "glimmer." I simply dip a toothpick into white or black gel paste and dab the "glimmer" to the figure's eyes.

MODELING FONDANT

Most tutorials included in this book require basic cutters and tools and rely greatly on modeling the fondant with your hands. You can easily work with fondant with a simple dip of your fingers in vegetable shortening to ensure it is malleable and with the knowledge of the following basic shapes: ball, oval, cone, square, rectangle and cylinder. In these tutorials I will also sometimes request that you roll out the fondant on your work surface, which basically resembles a piece of cooked spaghetti. Most figures that need to be modeled with your hands will originate from one of these shapes, so you can always refer back if necessary.

FONDANT GLUE

Since the simple addition of water turns fondant sticky, it's all you need to glue pieces together! I like to break up a bit of fondant into a bowl of water and mix it together for a glue. You can also mix a stronger glue by combining about 2 tablespoons warm water with ¼ teaspoon tylose powder until completely dissolved. Cover it and place it overnight in the refrigerator, which will cause it to become a clear, syrupy gel. Both glues can be stored in containers in the fridge, and while they can probably last indefinitely, I would rather be safe and only keep them for approximately a month, if that long.

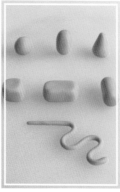

Fondant
CUTTERS & TOOLS

A s I continue to emphasize, the majority of the cupcake toppers included in this book require basic fondant tools that are easily accessible in baking, craft, and kitchen stores. The following is a review of basic-shaped cutters, tools, and materials needed for the simplest silhouettes to the construction of more elaborate designs.

CUTTERS

Many different types of cutters are available in the market, but the key is to look for the miniature shapes perfect for cupcake toppers; whether they are specifically intended for fondant or made for other treats (like cookies), whether they are metal or plastic—and as long as they are food safe— they can work with fondant! Sets of cutters can be a great investment and super useful when the need arises for the same shape in different sizes, as you will notice with the circle cutters in various measurements that originate from a twelve-piece set.

When prepping your work surface, make sure to sprinkle it with powdered sugar prior to rolling out the fondant and cutting the shapes out with the cutters, which ensures they don't stick. No matter how careful you are when cutting shapes out or coating the cutter with shortening, you will inevitably have "strays" (see p. 13). Take an extra minute with your fingers or tools to smooth the perimeter of the fondant shape to keep it nice and clean. Wipe off any leftover fondant from the cutter before you use it again. I keep paper towels on my worktable for this reason.

See next page for cutter photo references.

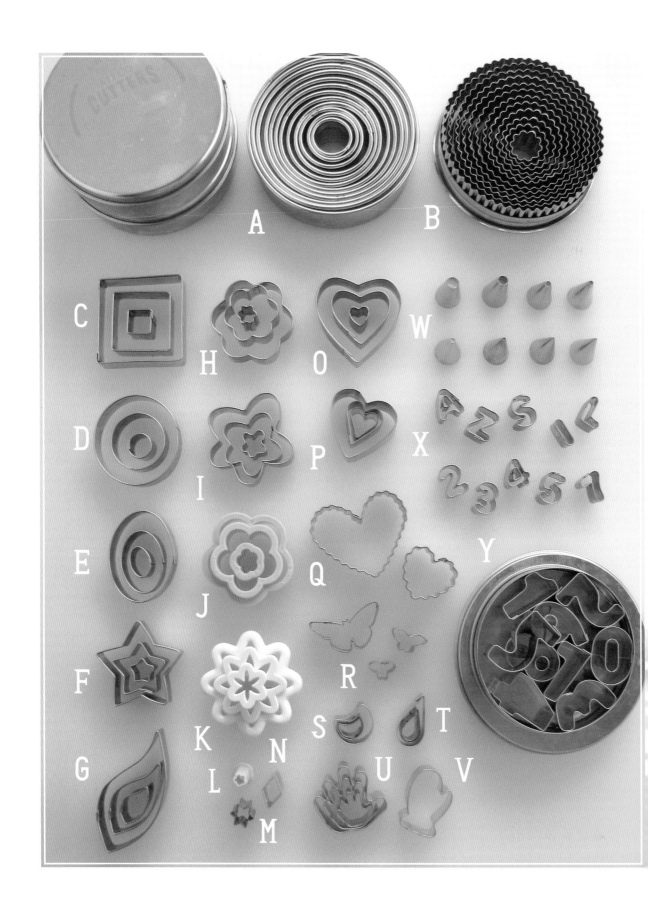

FONDANT CUTTERS

A) Circle cutters, 12-pc. set

B) Scalloped circle cutters, 12-pc. set

C) Square cutters, 3-pc. set

D) Circle cutters, 3-pc. set

E) Oval cutters, 3-pc. set

F) Star cutters, 3-pc. set

G) Leaf cutters, 3-pc. set

H) Flower cutters, 3-pc. set

I) Asymmetrical flower cutters, 3-pc. set

J) Plastic flower cutters, 3-pc. set

K) Plastic daisy cutters, 3-pc. set

L) Miniature flower cutter

M) Small hexagram cutter

N) Small diamond cutter

O) Heart cutters, 3-pc. set

P) Various-sized heart cutters

Q) Scalloped heart cutters

R) Various-sized butterfly cutters

S) Crescent cutters, 3-pc. set

T) Teardrop cutters, 3-pc. set

U) Hand cutters, 3-pc. set

V) Mitten cutter

W) Round tips (#s 1, 2, 3, 5, 6, 7, 10, 12)

X) Small letter and number cutter set

Y) Large number cutter set

CUTTER SUBSTITUTIONS

Although most cutters needed for the tutorials in this book are readily available in nationwide craft and baking stores as well as online shops, the following are some substitutions you can make with the less common shapes:

SCALLOP: Indent the perimeter of a circle with a knife tool.

FLOWER: Similar to the scallop shape, use the knife tool or precision knife to prominently indent the perimeter of a circle.

HANDS: Cut out a circle and use the knife tool to indent the fingers or a precision knife to cut the fingers out completely.

MITTEN: Use an oval cutter and trim the top and bottom with a precision knife in the shape of a mitten, while rounding out the top with your fingers.

BUTTERFLY: Cut out two heart shapes, turn them on their sides, trim the tips, and adjoin the ends with glue.

DIAMOND: Use a square cutter and trim it to a diamond shape with the sides of the square cutter or a precision knife.

TEARDROP: Modify an oval shape with a leaf cutter or trim one end with a precision knife to form the tip of the teardrop.

CRESCENT: Cut out a circle and use the same circle cutter to trim off the top.

Most shapes can be cut out of fondant with a precision knife, but the use of cutters is an extreme time-saver and will make your life so much easier! For example, the baby shower collections in this book contain instructions to cut out and form Onesies and bibs with the use of basic cutters, but you can also find these specific cutters on the market to allow you to simply punch out the shapes. Search for specific shapes you use most often, add them to your assortment, and substitute them within the tutorials.

CUTTER STORAGE AND ORGANIZATION

As you begin to accumulate cutters, storing them and finding the ones you need can be time-consuming! I use a combination of mason jars in various sizes and storage bins to keep my cutters separated into categories or themes. You can also create different types of labels to classify them. No matter what container I use, I make sure it is clear or see-through so I can easily spot what I need.

FONDANT TOOLS

The fondant tools used throughout the book are essential for rolling out fondant, shaping and cutting, and creating all the little details. They can be versatile and are used to execute and create different accents. Just like the cutters, they can be found in cake decorating and craft stores as well as online.

TOOLS

A) Thin foam mat and foam block

B) Flower-forming cup

C) Fondant storage board

D) Fondant embossing mats*

E) ¼-inch wooden dowels

F) Rolling pin and guide rings, $^1/_8$-inch and $^1/_{16}$-inch

G) Rolling pastry cutter

H) Precision knife

I) Knife tool

J) Modeling tool

K) Small modeling stick

L) Large modeling stick

M) Miniature ball tool

N) Small ball tool

O) Large ball tool

P) Veiner tool

Q) Brushes

R) Small spatulas

S) Food scissors

* Rose, dotted, linear, square, wood-grain, brick, honeycomb, damask, scroll

OTHER MATERIALS

These materials, while not specific to fondant, are extremely useful in shaping, embellishing, and securing fondant designs.

A) Parchment paper

B) Styrofoam block

C) Cardboard

D) Sharp knife

E) Toothpicks

F) Yellow, orange, and white stamen sets

G) Lollipop sticks

H) Raw spaghetti

I) Candy pearls, sprinkles, and sugars

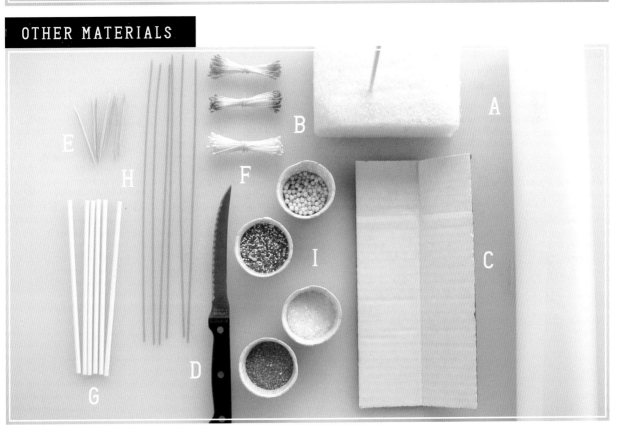

A B Q
F
C
D
E
S
M
J
R
G H
I
K L N O P

E
H
B
A
F
I
C
D
G

Fondant
TIPS & TECHNIQUES

While working on the cupcake toppers for this book, I made sure to note any recurring and crucial tips and techniques that would help you in executing any of the tutorials. The following are some key procedures to keep in mind.

ROLLING OUT FONDANT: Virtually every design will require you to roll out fondant with the rolling pin. You will note in the list of materials needed, as well as within the tutorial, that I will instruct you to roll out fondant one-eighth-inch thick, one-sixteenth-inch thick, or even more. While achieving these measurements might seem impossible, it is easily done with guide rings in the specific sizes that are inserted directly onto the rolling pin or by using one-fourth-inch wooden dowels as guides. These tools will make it simple to roll out uniform fondant pieces.

INDENTING: Many designs require some form of indentation using different tools. You might use a modeling stick to indent a circle or a round tip at a forty-five-degree angle to indent a mouth and smile. You can use a knife tool to make straight indentations or you might have to begin on one end and go up and over the fondant to indent fingers or wings. Pay close attention to the instructions and the detailed photos when making indentations. And remember to not wait long before indenting the fondant because if you do, it might have dried enough that it will crack or break and you'll have to start again!

LINT VS. FONDANT: This is a battle that plagues me every time I work with fondant! No matter how clean my work surface, tools, and hands are, when I start to roll a piece of fondant, lint appears out of nowhere! You can barely see it until it's stuck in your fondant, and it can be extremely aggravating. My advice would be to ensure the towel you use to dry your hands is lint-free, or better yet, use a paper towel. And before you start working with your fondant or adding color, use a small piece as the "sacrifice" fondant by rolling it in your hands and spreading it across your work surface to pick up every piece of undetectable lint. Hopefully fondant will be the winner in this match!

PERSONALIZING FONDANT: As mentioned previously, the easiest way to personalize the fondant designs in this book is to utilize initials and ages of the guest of honor or gift receiver. If I have specific ideas within each collection on how to customize a topper in relation to the theme, I will note in the "Personalize" section. But always keep in mind you can do this on your own with any design, utilizing alphabet and number cutters, making impressions with food-safe stamps, or writing with edible-ink markers or royal icing. No matter how you personalize, the receiver feels special when they know the toppers were made especially for them!

REMOVING FONDANT FROM THE CUTTERS: Often, when you use a cutter or a round metal tip to punch out a shape from the fondant, it gets stuck. Sometimes you can use your fingers to gently press them out without ruining the fondant or use a modeling tool to nudge it out. Since most of the time you won't see the back of the fondant piece on the final design, you can also use a precision knife to pull it out from behind; if you leave a mark, it won't be seen. When using decorating tips to cut out small circles, you can usually turn the tip around and tap it on your work surface. If it doesn't fall out then, you can use your fingers, a modeling stick, or a toothpick to gently nudge it out. And don't forget to run your fingers around the perimeter of the shape to get rid of "strays"!

ROLLING OUT

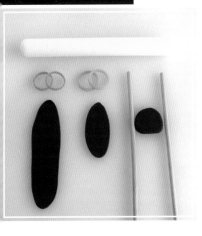

INDENTING

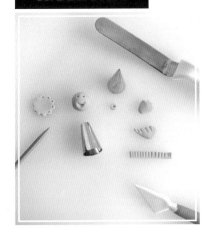

PERSONALIZING

REMOVING CUTTER

REMOVING STRAYS

Cupcakes

Nothing completes a celebration more than mouthwatering cupcakes, and the fondant toppers included in this book will make them the absolute center of attention. When it comes to the cupcakes, you have several options: homemade from scratch, from a box, or store-bought. Depending on the occasion and my schedule, I have done all three. It's truly a matter of preference, from the manner in which you bake or attain them to the flavor you choose. The possibilities are virtually endless. Whatever your choice for cupcakes is, the following are some tips and ideas to dress them up and prepare them to be topped.

When making my own cupcakes, I use an ice cream scoop with a release lever when pouring the batter into the liners. This makes it much easier to add them to the cupcake pan and ensure the cupcakes are all about the same size. Make sure you only fill the liners about three-fourths full so they don't overflow.

Many options are available for cupcake cups, liners, and wrappers to enhance your cupcake presentation. You can find thematic designs or matching color patterns that can coincide with your fondant toppers at craft stores, baking stores, and even grocery stores. You will find discerning the color or motif on some liners difficult once they are baked. If this is the case, you can add another liner to the cupcake after baking to register the look. Some companies also sell baking cups that are thicker or lined with foil to maintain the original coloration. You can also find wrappers that attach around your cupcake for different themes, such as grass, picket fences, or even graveyards. You can utilize the liners and wrappers with store-bought cupcakes as well.

If you are making cupcakes at home, there are several ways to frost them prior to adding your fondant toppers, depending on the design with which you are working. You can use a small spatula to spread the icing around the top of the cupcake or use frosting bags and decorating tips to achieve different patterns and effects, such as grass. Tint your frosting with gel pastes to match your theme or request specific frosting colors from your bakery when ordering.

Based on your design and theme, you can accentuate your cupcakes and frosting with various toppings. If your fondant topper does not take up the entire cupcake, you can add different sprinkles and sugars. In some cases, you can use crushed cookies to coat the top of the frosting, such as Oreo cookies for dirt or graham crackers for sand. The best way to crush them is to put the cookies (filling removed) or crackers in a ziplock bag. Make sure the bag is sealed and then use a rolling pin to roll over it back and forth until the cookies or crackers are completely crushed. And that's the way the cookie crumbles.

Fondant
CUPCAKE TOPPER TUTORIALS

Now that you're an expert on fondant, you're ready to try out the cupcake topper tutorials! Oh, don't worry—you don't have to be an expert at all. Just follow along, refer back to the tips as often as necessary, and, like my father always advises, have fun!

Please note: In addition to the specific materials, cutters, and tools listed in each collection, you will also need shortening and powdered sugar (p. 3) and fondant glue (p. 6).

PIECE OF CAKE

Materials Needed

fondant
(white, red, blue, yellow & brown)

raw spaghetti

lollipop stick

sharp knife

small block of Styrofoam

Cutters Needed

⅞-inch, 1⅞-inch & 2¼-inch circle cutters

small & medium flower cutters

#10 round tip

Tools Needed

rolling pin with ⅛-inch guide rings

rolling pastry cutter

knife tool

precision knife

Sweet Tips

SIMPLIFY	Omit the party hat and/or balloon and center the number on the cake.
ACCENTUATE	Make extra confetti and balloons to decorate additional cupcakes.
PERSONALIZE	Cut initials out of red, blue, and yellow fondant and place them directly on the frosting with extra fondant confetti or add them to the balloons.
EXPAND	Make additional cakes in different sizes and stack them up to make tiered levels.
DECORATE & DISPLAY	Include cupcake liners with bright, primary colors and use plenty of real balloons to decorate the table or fill them with helium and hang them behind the cupcakes.

Birthday Cake

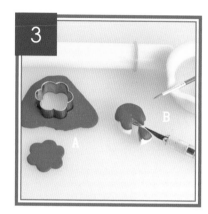

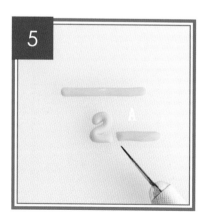

How to:

1. Using the rolling pin, roll out white and brown fondant ⅛ inch thick and cut out circles with the ⅞-inch cutter to make the cake layers (3 brown and 2 white) **(A)**. Glue them together **(B)**.

2. Roll out more white fondant ⅛ inch thick and use the 1⅞-inch circle cutter to cut out the cake cover **(A)**. Apply glue to the bottom and cover the layers of cake. Use the precision cutter to trim the excess **(B)**.

3. With the rolling pin, roll out red fondant ⅛ inch thick and cut out a medium flower shape with the cutter **(A)**. Glue it to the top of the covered cake and use the precision knife to cut out a slice **(B)**.

4. Roll blue fondant into a ball (approximately ½ inch) **(A)**. Then use your fingers to narrow one side of it to mold it into a cone shape. Roll out some yellow fondant ⅛ inch thick, cut out a small flower with the cutter, and glue it to the top of the party hat **(B)**.

5. To create the age candle, roll out yellow fondant with your fingers and mold the desired number, cutting off any excess with the knife **(A)**.

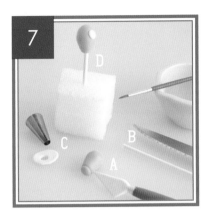

6. For the confetti, use the rolling pin to roll out fondant in various colors, each ⅛ inch thick. With the rolling pastry cutter, cut out strips **(A)**. Twist them around the raw spaghetti by holding 1 side of the strip down with 1 hand and rolling it around the spaghetti with the other. Allow confetti 5–10 minutes to dry sufficiently to hold their shape **(B)**.

7. Roll yellow fondant into a ball (approximately 1 inch) and begin to narrow one side of it enough to mold the bottom of a balloon. Utilize the knife tool to create a narrow crease around the edge of the balloon **(A)**. Use a sharp knife to cut a lollipop stick to the desired height (enough to fit into a cupcake and protrude from the topper) **(B)** and insert it into the bottom of the balloon. With the #10 round tip, cut a circle out of white fondant and with your fingers shape it into an oval **(C)**. Glue it onto the balloon and insert the stick into a Styrofoam block to dry **(D)**.

8. Roll out some white fondant ⅛ inch thick and use the 2¼-inch circle cutter to punch out a circle for the bottom **(A)**. With a lollipop stick, make a hole in the circle to later insert the balloon, once dry **(B)**. Glue all components of the topper together, including the cake, number candle, party hat, and confetti. Allow to dry thoroughly. Once completely dry, place the topper on a frosted cupcake and insert the balloon in the hole.

ONCE UPON A TIME

fondant
(pink & white)

edible shimmer/disco
dust & brushes

Cutters Needed

2¼-inch scalloped
circle cutter

small heart cutter

small star cutter

Tools Needed

rolling pin with
⅛-inch guide rings

knife tool

embossing mat

Sweet Tips

SIMPLIFY	Omit the crown from the princess pillow tutorial.
ACCENTUATE	Make larger wands and/or hearts brushed with shimmer dust to decorate additional cupcakes. Utilize the embossing mat for added texture.
PERSONALIZE	Cut out initials or ages from fondant and add larger princess wands for extra cupcakes. Or follow the tutorial to make the scrolls but shape them into letters or numbers instead.
EXPAND	Follow the bride tutorial from the Going to the Chapel collection (p. 236), replacing the white dress with a pink one for a princess.
DECORATE & DISPLAY	Display the princess cupcakes on bejeweled stands or candle holders. Brighten up the presentation with pearls, crystals, and tiaras found in the wedding section of craft stores. Tint your fondant pink to match.

Carriage

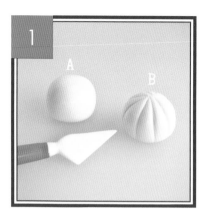

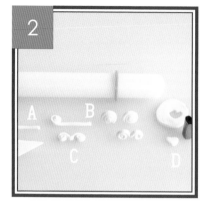

How to:

1. Roll white fondant into a ball (approximately 1½ inches) **(A)**. With the knife tool, start at the bottom of the ball and indent a line into the fondant all the way to the top. Create lines all around the ball with ¼ inch between each line **(B)**.

2. To make the carriage wheels, roll out white fondant with your fingers and cut four 3-inch strips with the knife tool **(A)**. Start at one end and coil the strip into itself. Stand the wheels upright to allow them to dry **(B)**. For the adornment at the top of the carriage, roll out another piece of white fondant and cut it into a 3-inch strip. Make an indent in the middle of the strip with the knife tool and coil both ends downward until they meet the center **(C)**. Cut a small heart out of white fondant for the doorway **(D)**.

3. With a brush, spread shimmer dust over all pieces of the carriage and glue the pieces together.

4. With a rolling pin, roll out pink fondant ⅛ inch thick and spread a bit of shortening over the fondant. Place the embossing mat over the fondant and use the rolling pin to impress the pattern onto it. Use the 2¼-inch scalloped cutter to punch out a circle and glue the carriage in the center. Allow to dry thoroughly.

Princess Pillow

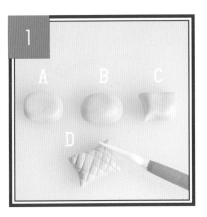

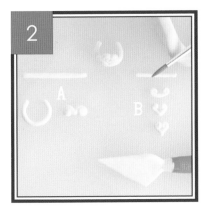

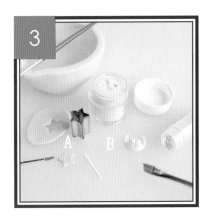

How to:

1. Roll pink fondant into a ball (approximately 1 inch) and shape it into a rectangle with your fingers (**A**). Round out all four sides of the rectangle with the tip of your finger (**B**) and then pinch all four corners (**C**). With the knife tool, create diagonal indentations across the pillow and repeat going the opposite way (**D**).

2. Roll out 2 strips of white fondant with your fingers and cut them to 1½ inches. Twist one of the strips into a horseshoe shape and create the first tiara adornment by indenting the other strip in the middle with the knife tool and coiling the sides downward (**A**). Roll out another white strip of fondant and cut it to 1 inch. Indent the middle with the knife tool and coil both ends upward until they meet, creating a heart shape. Pinch the end with your fingers (**B**). Glue the tiara pieces together.

3. Roll out some pink fondant ⅛ inch thick and cut out a small star (**A**). For the wand, with your fingers, roll out white fondant with your fingers into an approximately 1-inch strip. Brush shimmer/disco dust on the tiara and star and, once the star has hardened a bit, glue the star onto the wand (**B**).

4. With the rolling pin, roll out white fondant ⅛ inch thick, spread some shortening over it, and impress the pattern with the embossing mat. Cut out a circle with the 2¼-inch scalloped cutter and glue all components together. Allow to dry thoroughly.

PIXIE DUST

fondant
(pink, green & brown)

pink & green
shimmer dust
& brushes

foam block

cardboard &
parchment paper

round tips #7 & #10

butterfly cutters
(various sizes)

small leaf cutter

rolling pin with
⅛-inch guide rings

knife tool

embossing mat

Sweet Tips

SIMPLIFY	Omit the fairy house and simply frost your cupcake tall and decorate with butterflies.
ACCENTUATE	In addition to the extra butterflies, cut out two-dimensional silhouettes and simply brush with shimmer dust.
PERSONALIZE	Form initials or ages to look like scrolling branches. Or emboss and cut out initials or ages and glue small butterflies on them.
EXPAND	Follow the wand tutorial from the Once upon a Time collection (p. 25) to make fairy wands in green and pink colorways. Instead of stars, you can replace them with small butterflies.
DECORATE & DISPLAY	Use grass liners or wrappers to adorn your cupcakes and give it an outdoor look. Tint your frosting green to resemble grass as well.

Butterfly & Fairy Home

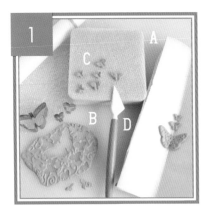

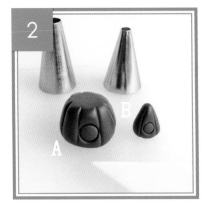

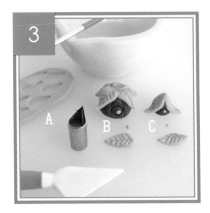

How to:

1. Fold the piece of cardboard in the middle lengthwise and line it with parchment paper **(A)**. With the rolling pin, roll out green and pink fondant ⅛ inch thick, spread shortening over it, and impress it with the embossing mat. Punch out various butterfly sizes with the cutters **(B)**. Place the smaller butterflies on the foam block and utilize the knife tool to indent their middles **(C)**. Center all the butterflies down the cardboard piece with their wings folding upward and allow them to dry 10–12 hours **(D)**.

2. Roll a piece of brown fondant into a ball (approximately 1 inch) and flatten out the top and bottom while narrowing the top a bit more. With the knife tool, make vertical indentations around the perimeter. Use round tip #10 to indent the front for the door **(A)**. Roll a smaller piece of brown fondant into a ball (approximately ⅓ inch) and shape it into a cone for the second floor. With the knife tool, make vertical indentations from the bottom to the tip of the cone. Use round tip #7 to indent the front window **(B)**.

3. With the rolling pin, roll out green fondant ⅛ inch thick and cut out 7 small leaf shapes with the cutter **(A)**. Pinch 3 of the leaves at their rounded ends to make them pointed. Using the knife tool, indent the middle of the leaves lengthwise and then

indent with small diagonal lines for the leaf veins. Glue the rounded leaves to the larger, bottom layer of the house with the pointed sides facing out **(B)**. Glue the rest of the leaves to the second floor of the house, joining the pinched sides at the top of the cone **(C)**. Roll small pieces of green fondant into balls, flatten them out with your finger, and glue them onto the door and window respectively.

4. Brush the pink and green shimmer dust onto the butterflies **(A)**. Glue a couple of small butterflies to the fairy house and glue the second floor on top of the bottom of the house **(B)**. Once thoroughly dried, utilize the rest of the butterflies to decorate frosted cupcakes.

ALL DOLLED UP

Materials Needed

fondant
(pink, white & light gray)

silver shimmer
dust & brush

Cutters Needed

2¼-inch scalloped
circle cutter

⅞-inch circle cutter

small asymmetrical
flower cutter

Tools Needed

rolling pin with
⅛-inch guide rings

2 wooden dowels

knife tool

modeling stick

Sweet Tips

SIMPLIFY
Reduce the number of makeup tools on each topper. You can also simply glue the nail polish top to the bottle and avoid making the brush and spilled polish.

ACCENTUATE
Cut out fondant pieces with the larger asymmetrical flower cutters to decorate additional cupcakes as nail polish colors.

PERSONALIZE
Make additional initials and ages to decorate more cupcakes in pink and silver.

EXPAND
Follow the tutorial for the sleep mask in the Glam Sleepover collection (p. 38) in a simple silver or pink combination to add to the assortment.

DECORATE & DISPLAY
Utilize girly plates, compacts, and makeup tools to display your beauty cupcakes.

31

Nail Polish

How to:

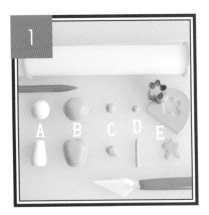

1. Roll some white fondant into a ball (approximately ½ inch) and mold the top of a nail polish bottle with your fingers, narrowing at the top and flattening out both the top and bottom. Use the modeling stick to insert a hole at the bottom by slowly twisting it into the fondant **(A)**. Roll pink fondant into a ball (approximately 1 inch) and mold the nail polish bottle, narrowing the bottom and then creating an indent along the bottom with the knife tool. With the modeling stick, make a hole at the top of the bottle by slowly twisting it into the fondant **(B)**. Roll some pink fondant into a ball (approximately ¼ inch) and form it into a teardrop to make the brush. Use the knife tool to indent lines and the modeling stick to insert a hole at the wider end **(C)**. Roll some pink fondant into a ball (approximately ⅛ inch) and roll it out with your fingers to make a stick **(D)**. Use the rolling pin to roll out pink fondant ⅛ inch thick and then cut out a small asymmetrical flower. Flatten it out a bit with your fingers to create the spilled nail polish **(E)**.

2. With the rolling pin, roll out the light gray fondant ⅛ inch thick and use the 2¼-inch scalloped cutter to punch out a circle **(A)**. Roll out more light gray fondant with your hands and mold an "N," a small circle, and a number for the desired age with your fingers **(B)**. Use the brush to spread silver shimmer dust over the light gray fondant pieces **(C)**. Glue all pieces together. Allow to dry thoroughly.

Makeup

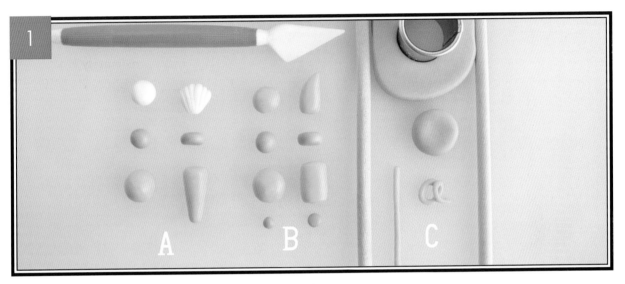

1

A   B   C

How to:

1. To create the makeup brush, roll white fondant into a ball (approximately $^3/_8$ inch) and shape it into a triangle. Using the knife tool, start at the very bottom and make indentations, making sure to follow the lines all the way up and over the top to create brush creases. Flatten the bottom a bit so that it ends up looking like a shell. Roll light gray fondant into a ball (approximately ¼ inch) and flatten it out a bit. Roll pink fondant into a ball (approximately ½ inch) and shape it into a long cone to make the bottom of the brush **(A)**.

   To make the lipstick, roll more pink fondant into a ball (approximately $^3/_8$ inch). Shape it into a cylinder and then flatten the top diagonally to form the top of a lipstick. Roll light gray fondant into a ball (approximately ¼ inch) and flatten it out a bit. Roll pink fondant into a ball (approximately $^5/_8$ inch) and shape it into a cylinder. Roll a small piece of light gray fondant into a ball (approximately $^1/_8$ inch) and flatten it with your finger **(B)**.

   To make the compact, roll out light gray fondant thick with the rolling pin and wooden dowels. Use the $^7/_8$-inch circle cutter to punch out a circle. With your fingers, round out the edge of the circle and use the knife tool to indent the side of the circle. Roll out pink fondant with your fingers and shape it to the desired letter **(C)**. Brush silver shimmer on all the light gray pieces. With the rolling pin, roll out white fondant $^1/_8$ inch thick and cut out a circle with the 2¼-inch scalloped cutter. Glue everything together and allow to dry thoroughly.

GLAM SLEEPOVER

4.

Materials Needed

fondant
(black, white & hot pink)

yellow gel paste

copper shimmer dust

Cutters Needed

2¼-inch scalloped
circle cutter

⅞-inch circle cutter

round tips
#7 & #10

small oval cutter

medium heart cutter

Tools Needed

rolling pin with
⅛-inch guide rings

2 wooden dowels

rolling pastry cutter

precision knife

rounded modeling tool

small modeling stick

small & large ball tools

foam block

knife tool

Sweet Tips

SIMPLIFY	Instead of a zebra print, make solid-colored sleeping bags and masks. Omit the pajamas and popcorn.
ACCENTUATE	Decorate additional toppers entirely with the zebra print. Make larger slippers with fuzzy pom-poms.
PERSONALIZE	Make larger pillows and add initials or ages to look like they are monogrammed.
EXPAND	Follow the tutorials for makeup or nail polish from the All Dolled Up collection (p. 31) to match the pink and zebra-print theme.
DECORATE & DISPLAY	Utilize zebra-print cupcake liners and accentuate with hot pink frosting. Utilize zebra platters and popcorn to decorate your presentation.

Candy

LEVEL OF DIFFICULTY

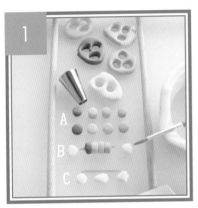

How to:

1. Using the rolling pin and wooden dowels as guides, roll out white, pink, yellow, light blue, and purple fondant thick. Cut out circles in the colored fondant with round tip #10 and flatten them out just a bit **(A)**. Cut a piece of raw spaghetti (approximately 1¼ inch) and thread through 4 colored circles to form the candy roll **(B)**. Cut out 2 circles in the white fondant with round tip #10 and form them into teardrops. With the knife tool, make 2 indentations in the wider side **(C)**. Glue them onto the ends of the spaghetti.

2. Use the rolling pin and wooden dowels to roll out fondant in the desired color thick, along with white. Use the large end of round tip #3 to cut out the candy and use your fingers and shortening to round out the sides **(A)**. Use the leaf cutter to cut out 2 pieces of white fondant, and, with the knife tool, make 2 indentations on the end of the wide side and flatten out the pointed end. Glue them onto the candy on opposite sides of each other **(B)**. With the rolling pin, roll out white fondant ⅛ inch thick and, with round tip #3, cut out small circles to embellish the candy **(C)**. For the gumdrops, use the rolling pin to roll out the desired color of fondant ⅛ inch thick. Use the large end of round tip #3 to cut out circles and roll them into balls **(D)**. Use your fingers and shortening to narrow the tops a bit, but make sure they remain rounded **(E)**. Roll out light blue fondant with the rolling pin ⅛ inch thick and use the 2¼-inch scalloped cutter to punch out the bottom topper. Use round tip #1 to punch out little holes around the scalloped ends to create an eyelet effect. Glue all pieces together. Allow to dry thoroughly.

Sweet Tooth

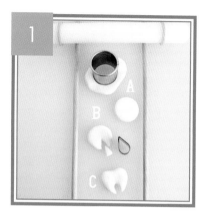

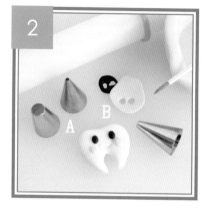

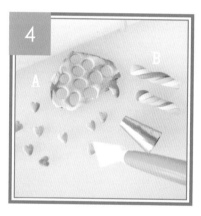

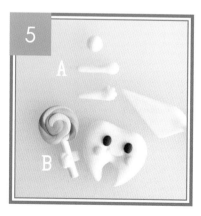

How to:

1. Using the wooden dowels and rolling pin, roll out some white fondant thick and cut out a circle with the 1¼-inch cutter **(A)**. Cut a small slice out of the circle with the leaf cutter **(B)** and use your fingers with some shortening to shape the bottom of the tooth as well as indent the center at the top **(C)**.

2. For the tooth's mouth, hold round tip #10 out at a 45-degree angle and make an indent in the tooth. Use round tip #3 to indent little dimples (inward-facing) at the ends of the mouth **(A)**. Roll out pink and black fondant with the rolling pin ⅛ inch thick and cut out 2 circles of each color with round tip #7. Shape the black to form an oval and glue onto the tooth for eyes. Glue on the pink circles for the cheeks **(B)**.

3. Roll out strips of the 4 colors of fondant (purple, yellow, pink, and light blue) with your fingers, approximately the same length. Lay the strips on the table next to each other and take one end of the first color and twist it over the 4 colors. Repeat with the remaining colors and then hold both ends of all 4 colors and begin to twist **(A)**. Once twisted, place it on the table and roll it to blend the colors and make one piece with all 4 colors **(B)**. To make the lollipop, cut off and discard the end of the colored braid and begin rolling the fondant piece into itself to the desired size **(C)**. Use the sharp knife to cut the lollipop stick and insert into the lollipop **(D)**.

4. With the excess colors, make small marbled hearts and marshmallow twists: make sure to set aside the colors you will utilize for both the hearts and the twists since different techniques will be used for both. For the hearts, combine the colors together and then roll the fondant flat with the rolling pin and cut out circles with round tip #10. Pinch the bottoms together and use the knife tool to indent the tops, forming a small heart **(A)**. To make a marshmallow twist, repeat the process of the colored braid, but don't roll it super tight **(B)**.

5. Roll white fondant into a ball (approximately ¼ inch) and begin to roll it out on the table, leaving one end more full. Use the knife tool to make four indentations on the full end to form the hand **(A)**. Mold the arm around the lollipop stick and cut off the excess of the arm at the desired length to glue to the tooth **(B)**. Roll out light blue fondant with the rolling pin ⅛ inch thick and use the 2¼-inch scalloped cutter to punch out the bottom topper. Use round tip #1 to punch out little holes around the scalloped ends to create an eyelet effect. Glue all pieces together. Allow to dry thoroughly.

BAKED WITH LOVE

Materials Needed

fondant
(pink, light blue, white & 2 shades of brown)

Cutters Needed

1¼-inch, 1½-inch & 2¼-inch scalloped circle cutters

round tips #1 & #10

small heart cutter

small flower cutter

mitten cutter

medium scalloped heart cutter
(regular heart cutter will work if you don't have scalloped)

Tools Needed

rolling pin with ⅛-inch guide rings

rolling pastry cutter

knife tool

small modeling stick

dotted embossing mat

foam block

Sweet Tips

SIMPLIFY	Omit the frosting bag from the Cut-Out Cookies tutorial. Use small heart decorations rather than flowers on the apron and chef hat.
ACCENTUATE	Make more cut-out cookies and oven mitts to accentuate additional cupcakes. Cut simple shapes out of the light brown fondant to represent baked cookies.
PERSONALIZE	Cut numbers or initials out of the light brown fondant to resemble cut-out cookies. Or roll out white fondant with your fingers and mold it into numbers, letters, or words to resemble frosting.
EXPAND	Follow the lollipop tutorial from the Sweet Tooth collection (p. 42) to combine several colors and make swirled frosting to add to the cookies and additional toppers.
DECORATE & DISPLAY	Use simple baking supplies, such as rolling pins, spatulas, and cute bakery boxes, to complete your presentation.

Cut-Out Cookies

LEVEL OF DIFFICULTY

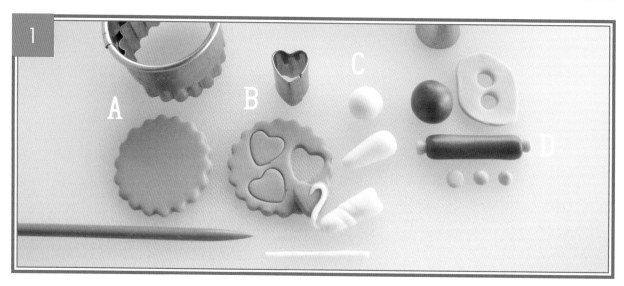

How to:

1. With the rolling pin, roll out the light brown fondant and use the 1½-inch scalloped cutter to punch out a circle **(A)**. With the small heart cutter, indent two heart shapes in the circle and punch out one small heart completely **(B)**. Roll white fondant into a ball (approximately ⅓ inch) and, with your fingers and shortening, form the ball into a cone shape. Hold the two ends and twist it in the center a bit. Use the small modeling stick to make a small hole on the tip and a larger hole at the end. Roll out white fondant with your fingers and begin to "frost" the cut-out cookie and glue the other end of the frosting into the small tip of the frosting bag **(C)**. For the fondant rolling pin, roll the darker brown fondant into a ball (approximately ½ inch) and, with your fingers, roll it out on the table to elongate it. Use the small modeling stick to make holes at both ends. With a rolling pin, roll out pink fondant ⅛ inch thick and punch out 2 small circles with round tip #10. Roll them into balls and then into cones and glue the pointed sides into the holes of the fondant rolling pin **(D)**. With a rolling pin, roll out light blue fondant ⅛ inch thick and spread a bit of shortening over the fondant. Place the embossing mat over the fondant and use the rolling pin to impress the pattern onto it. Use the 2¼-inch scalloped cutter to punch out a circle in the fondant. With round tip #1, make holes around the perimeter of the scalloped circle. Utilize the small modeling stick to round out and clean up each hole. Glue all the pieces together. Allow to dry thoroughly.

Chef Tools

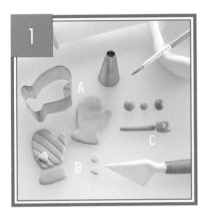

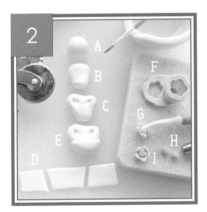

How to:

1. With the rolling pin, roll out light blue fondant ⅛ inch thick and punch out a mitten shape with the cutter. Cut off the very end to resemble an oven mitt and use the knife tool to make linear indentations in the mitt (**A**). (If you don't have a mitten cutter, use a medium-sized oval cutter and trim the top and bottom with a precision knife in the shape of an oven mitt.) With the rolling pin, roll out pink fondant ⅛ inch thick and cut out a circle with round tip #10. Pinch one end together and use the knife tool to indent the opposite end to create a small heart (**B**). Glue the heart onto the oven mitt. For the baking spatula, roll out light blue and light brown fondant into balls (approximately ¼ inch) and roll out a smaller light blue ball. Flatten the smaller blue ball onto the bigger blue ball. Roll out the light brown fondant into a handle and glue pieces together (**C**).

2. For the chef hat, roll white fondant into a ball (approximately ¾ inch) (**A**). With your fingers and shortening, shape the ball a bit flatter and narrow one end (**B**). Make an indent at the top of the hat with your fingers, making one side a bit larger than the other. Use the small ball tool to indent the front on both sides (**C**). With the rolling pin, roll out white fondant ⅛ inch thick and, with the rolling pastry cutter, cut out a strip ¾ inches wide. Measure it against the chef hat, trim both sides diagonally (**D**), and glue it to the bottom of the hat, wrapping it around and underneath (**E**). To create the accent flower, with the rolling pin roll out pink fondant ⅛ inch thick and cut out a flower with the small cutter (**F**). On the foam block, use the small ball tool in the middle of the flower, which will bring the petals upward (**G**). Roll out a small piece of light blue fondant and cut out a circle with round tip #10. Pinch one end together and use the knife tool to indent the opposite end to create a small heart (**H**). Glue the heart in the center of the flower (**I**) and glue the flower onto the bottom side of the chef hat. With a rolling pin, roll out pink fondant ⅛ inch thick and spread a bit of shortening over the fondant. Place the embossing mat over the fondant and use the rolling pin to impress the pattern onto it. Use the 2¼-inch scalloped cutter to punch out a circle. With round tip #1, make holes around the perimeter of the scalloped circle. Utilize the small modeling stick to round out and clean up each hole. Glue all the pieces together. Allow to dry thoroughly.

Apron

How to:

1. Roll out pink fondant with the rolling pin ⅛ inch thick and cut out a medium scalloped heart and 1½-inch scalloped circle with the respective cutters. Use the bottom of the heart cutter to trim the top of the circle so the 2 fondant pieces will fit together **(A)**. Glue them together. With the rolling pin, roll out white fondant ⅛ inch thick and cut out a circle with the 1¼-inch scalloped cutter. With the rolling pastry cutter, trim a piece off the top of the white circle. Push the top center of the larger white piece down with your fingers so it droops. Glue it to the pink apron **(B)**. Follow the chef tools tutorial (p. 47) to make another flower (in this case with the light blue fondant and replacing the inner heart with a smaller flower) and 2 small hearts. Glue these to the apron **(C)**. Use the small modeling stick to make indentations for the seams around the perimeter of the apron (on both the pink and white layers) **(D)**. Allow to dry thoroughly.

WHAT A HOOT

Materials Needed

fondant
(brown, light blue, white, orange & black)

raw spaghetti

tylose powder

Cutters Needed

$\frac{7}{8}$-inch circle cutter

$1\frac{7}{8}$-inch scalloped circle cutter

round tips #10 & #12

small circle cutter

medium leaf cutter

Tools Needed

rolling pin with $\frac{1}{8}$-inch guide rings

knife tool

rounded modeling tool

Sweet Tips

SIMPLIFY	Don't make the indentations on the eyes, belly, and wings.
ACCENTUATE	Decorate additional cupcakes with simple owl eyes or leaves.
PERSONALIZE	Form initials or ages with scrolling branches.
EXPAND	Follow the tutorial for baby chicks from the Down on the Farm collection (p. 57) to make baby owls or add books from the Bookworm collection (p. 157) to make it a wise owl.
DECORATE & DISPLAY	Utilize wood and natural accents, such as pinecones and acorns, to embellish your presentation. Nests and birdhouses make great props!

Owl

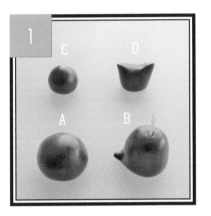

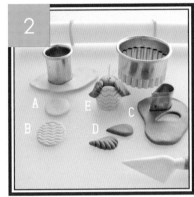

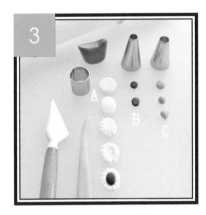

How to:

1. Knead tylose powder into the brown fondant and roll it into a ball (approximately 1 inch) **(A)**. With shortening and your fingers, roll the ball into a cylindrical shape, narrowing toward the top and pinching a little piece together in the back to form a little tail. Insert a piece of raw spaghetti into the center, sticking out enough to fit into the head **(B)**. Roll a second piece of brown fondant into a ball (approximately ¾ inch) for the head **(C)**. Use your fingers dipped in shortening to pinch 2 sides together to form the ears. Round out the top center of the head **(D)**. Fit the head onto the body through the protruding spaghetti to ensure it fits properly.

2. With the rolling pin, roll out light blue fondant ⅛ inch thick and punch out a circle using the ⅞-inch cutter **(A)**. Elongate it a bit to make it into an oval and use the 1⅞-inch scalloped cutter to indent the pattern **(B)**. Glue it onto the front of the owl. With the rolling pin, roll out brown fondant ⅛ inch thick and cut out 2 wings with the medium leaf cutter **(C)**. With the knife tool, indent diagonal lines from the inside of the wings upward toward the broader end **(D)**. Glue the wings onto the owl with the ends shaped out **(E)**.

(continued on next page)

(continued):

3. With the rolling pin, roll out white fondant ⅛ inch thick and cut out 2 circles with the small circle cutter. Shape the circle into an oval and use the knife tool to indent around the sides, leaving a smaller oval shape in the center to create the eyes. Use the rounded modeling tool to indent the center oval **(A)**. With the rolling pin, roll out black fondant ⅛ inch thick and cut out 2 circles with round tip #10 **(B)**. Shape the circles into small ovals and glue them to the center of the white eyes. Roll out orange fondant with the rolling pin ⅛ inch thick and cut out a circle with round tip #12. Roll it into a ball and pinch one end together to create the beak **(C)**. Glue the eyes and beak to the owl.

4. With the rolling pin, roll out orange fondant ⅛ inch thick and cut out 2 circles with round tip #12. Roll each circle into a ball and pinch one end. Use the knife tool to indent the fuller ends to create the feet **(A)**. Glue the feet to the front of the owl. With the rolling pin, roll out light blue fondant ⅛ inch thick and cut out 3 circles with round tip #10. Roll all 3 circles into balls. Shape 2 of them into teardrops and indent the middles with the rounded modeling tool. Glue the 2 tips to the remaining ball to form the bow **(B)**. Glue the bow onto the owl's head and glue the head onto the body, inserting it through the protruding raw spaghetti.

DOWN ON THE FARM

Materials Needed

fondant
(light brown, dark brown, black, ivory, light gray, pink, white, red & yellow)

raw spaghetti

silver shimmer
dust & brush

tylose powder

Cutters Needed

round tips
#3, #10 & #12

small oval cutter

small circle cutter

small star cutter

small teardrop cutter

Tools Needed

rolling pin with
⅛-inch guide rings

2 wooden dowels

knife tool

modeling tool

small modeling stick

food scissors

Sweet Tips

SIMPLIFY	Avoid adding the extra accessories on the horse.
ACCENTUATE	Cut out larger stars and horseshoes to decorate additional cupcakes. Use medium and large leaf cutters to make paisley toppers.
PERSONALIZE	Use the rope technique to mold various rope shapes, initials, or ages.
EXPAND	Follow the tutorial for cowboy hats from the Western Trails collection (p. 60) to add to the farm.
DECORATE & DISPLAY	Use green frosting and decorating tip #233 to make grass, crushed graham crackers or toasted coconut for the ground, and chocolate frosting for mud. Decorate your presentation with small hay bales, horseshoes, and western scarves.

Horse

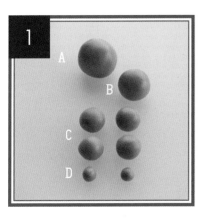

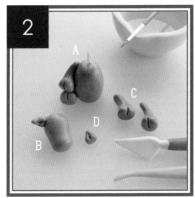

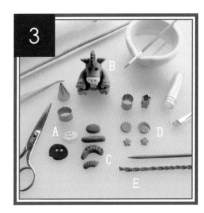

How to:

1. Knead tylose powder into the light brown fondant. Then roll the fondant into balls as follows: body, 1¼-inch **(A)**; head, ¾-inch **(B)**; 4 limbs, ½-inch **(C)**; 2 ears, ⅜-inch **(D)**.

2. Roll out the body into an oval shape and place it on your work surface. Insert a raw spaghetti with enough protruding to hold the head **(A)**. Roll the head into an oval and narrow one side for the snout. Make sure to fit the head through the spaghetti before it begins to dry **(B)**. Roll out the limbs, keeping one end thick and proportionally narrowing the rest of the arms and legs, forming it around the horse's body. Flatten the horse's hooves and, with the knife tool, indent the top **(C)** and glue the limbs onto the body. Shape the small fondant balls into cone shapes and, with the modeling tool, indent the middle of the ears. Pinch the pointed end together **(D)** and glue the ears to the horse's head.

3. With the rolling pin, roll out ivory fondant ⅛ inch thick and cut out a small oval. Use the bottom of round tip #3 to create an indent at a 45-degree angle for the mouth. Use the modeling tool to make 2 indentations for the nostrils **(A)** and glue it to the horse's snout. With the rolling pin, roll out black fondant ⅛ inch thick. Cut out 2 eyes with round tip #3 and glue them to the head **(B)**. Roll out the dark brown fondant with the rolling pin and wooden dowels and cut out a small oval with the oval cutter. Roll it out a bit longer with your fingers and use the food scissors to make cuts along one entire side, creating the horse's mane. Repeat with a smaller piece for the tail **(C)** and glue these on the horse. Roll out light gray fondant with the rolling pin ⅛ inch thick and cut out 4 small circles and 1 small star with the respective cutters. Use the small oval cutter to cut out a piece of each of the circles, creating a horseshoe shape. With the small modeling stick, create a pattern on the horseshoe and the perimeter of the star. Brush silver shimmer dust over them **(D)**. Roll out 2 pieces of red fondant into long, thin lines (approximately 7 inches) and twist them together, creating a rope **(E)**. Glue the rope wrapped around the horse's head, creating a lanyard, and add the silver star to the middle. Glue the horseshoes onto the horse's hooves and the head onto the body and allow to dry thoroughly.

Pig

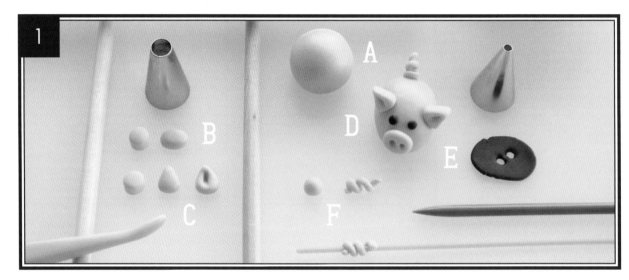

How to:

1. Roll pink fondant into a 1-inch ball and shape it into an oval with your fingers to create the pig's body **(A)**. With the small modeling stick, indent the pig's behind to later insert the tail. Roll out pink fondant thick with the rolling pin and wooden dowels. Use round tip #12 to cut out 3 circles. Round 1 of the circles out into an oval shape to create the pig's snout **(B)**. Shape the other 2 into cone shapes and use the modeling tool to indent the centers of the ears **(C)**. Glue the ears and snout to the pig and, with the small modeling stick, create 2 indents in the snout **(D)**. With the rolling pin, roll out black fondant ⅛ inch thick and use round tip #3 to cut out 2 eyes **(E)**. Glue the eyes to the pig. Roll out pink fondant into a thin strip and roll it around the raw spaghetti **(F)**. Allow the tail to dry for a few minutes to retain the spiral shape and then insert it into the pig's behind, gluing the tail. Allow to dry thoroughly. To create the pig's behind sticking out of the mud, roll out pink fondant thick with the rolling pin and wooden dowels. Use the larger end of a round tip to punch out a circle and round tip #12 to cut out 2 small circles. Round out the perimeter of the larger circle with your fingers and use the small modeling stick to make a hole for the tail. Repeat the steps above to form and glue the tail. Round out the 2 remaining small circles into ovals and utilize the knife tool to indent each end to form the pig hooves. Glue them in place and allow to dry thoroughly.

Chicken

How to:

1. Roll white fondant into a 1-inch ball and use your fingers to shape it into an oval. Narrow the top for the head. Angle it onto the work surface so it leans forward a bit **(A)**. With the rolling pin, roll out white fondant ⅛ inch thick and use the small teardrop cutter to cut out 2 wings. Use the knife tool to indent the tops of the wings **(B)**. Glue them onto the chicken. With the rolling pin and wooden dowels, roll out red fondant thick and cut out a small teardrop shape. Smooth it out with your fingers and use the food scissors to make cuts down one side to create the chicken's comb **(C)**. Glue it onto the head. With the rolling pin, roll out yellow fondant ⅛ inch thick and create a cone shape for the beak **(D)**. Glue the beak to the chicken. With the rolling pin, roll out black fondant ⅛ inch thick, cut out 2 eyes with round tip #3 **(E)**, and glue them onto the chicken. Allow to dry thoroughly. Repeat steps on a smaller scale to create little chicks, using yellow fondant for the bodies, red fondant for the beaks, and omitting the wings and comb.

WESTERN TRAILS

Materials Needed

fondant
(brown, ivory, turquoise & green)

raw spaghetti

Cutters Needed

1½-inch circle cutter

round tip #10

small leaf cutter

Tools Needed

rolling pin with
⅛-inch guide rings

2 wooden dowels

knife tool

precision knife

modeling tool

small modeling stick

food scissors

Sweet Tips

SIMPLIFY	Omit the additional decorations on the cowboy hat.
ACCENTUATE	Use a star cutter to cut out sheriff badges. Or use the leaf cutter and embossing mat to create paisley shapes to embellish additional cupcakes.
PERSONALIZE	Use the rope technique to mold them into various rope shapes, initials, or ages. Or add initials or ages to larger sheriff badges.
EXPAND	Add animal fondant toppers from the Down on the Farm collection (p. 53).
DECORATE & DISPLAY	Utilize wood, horn, and pottery elements for decoration and coat your cupcakes with frosting and crushed graham crackers for edible sand.

Cowboy Hat

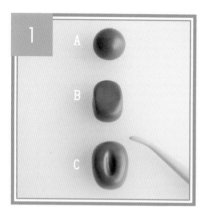

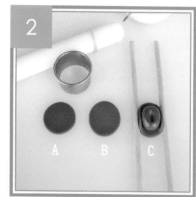

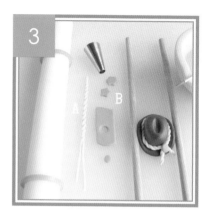

How to:

1. Roll out brown fondant into a ball (approximately 1 inch) **(A)** and shape it into a rectangle **(B)**. Use your fingers dipped in shortening to round out the sides. With the modeling tool, create an indent in the center of the hat **(C)**.

2. With the rolling pin, roll out brown fondant ⅛ inch thick and use the 1½-inch cutter to punch out a circle **(A)**. Pull opposite ends of the circle apart just a bit to make it more oval **(B)**. Place the top of the hat in the center of the oval and flip the 2 narrower sides of the brim up. Use the 2 wooden dowels to hold them up to dry **(C)**. If not adding embellishments, glue the hat to the brim. If adding a trim, move on to the next step prior to gluing—it is easier to attach the trim first and mold the brim around it.

3. Very thinly roll out 2 strips of ivory fondant with your fingers. Hold the 2 pieces together at one end with one hand, and, with the other hand, twist the 2 pieces together to create a rope for the hat trim **(A)**. Glue the rope to the hat and cut off the excess with the precision knife. Use the rolling pin to roll out turquoise fondant ⅛ inch thick. Use round tip #10 to cut out a circle. Shape it into an oval and glue it to the rope **(B)**. Use different shaped cutters, such as stars or flowers, to create additional embellishments. Once decorations have been added, glue the hat to the brim and allow to dry thoroughly.

Steer Head

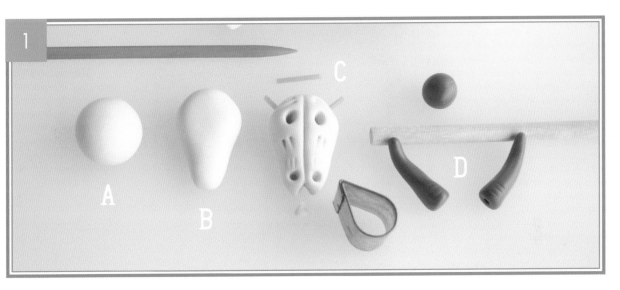

How to:

1. Roll ivory fondant into a ball (approximately 1 inch) **(A)**. Use your fingers to mold the steer head, narrowing the bottom of the ball and flattening out the 2 top sides of the head where the horns will go **(B)**. Cut out a small piece at the bottom of the head with the tip of the leaf cutter. Using the knife tool and small modeling stick, create the skeleton indentations. Insert 2 pieces of raw spaghetti where the horns will go to hold them securely in place **(C)**. Roll brown fondant into 2 balls (approximately ⅓ inch) and shape each into a cone. Hold the tip with your fingers and twist it upward, ensuring the 2 horns are in opposite directions. Insert raw spaghetti into the larger ends to make holes where they will be inserted into the steer head. Use the knife tool to create markings on the horns. Lean them up against the wooden dowel to allow them to dry a bit. Insert them into the raw spaghetti in the steer head and glue them together **(D)**.

Cactus

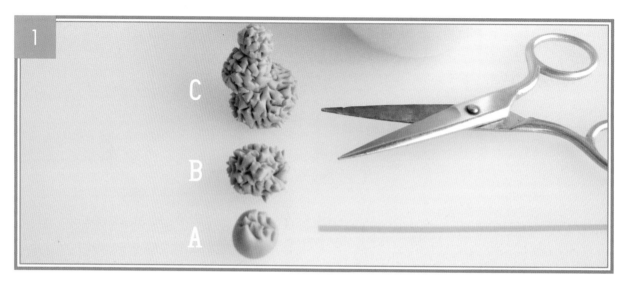

How to:

1. Roll green fondant into different-sized balls and use the food scissors to make small cuts around the entire area (**A**), varying the directions but making sure you do not cut off the fondant completely (**B**). Insert a raw spaghetti into smaller pieces to make it is easier to hold while cutting and remove it when drying. Be creative when gluing the pieces together, making small and large cactus designs (**C**).

QUEEN BEE

Materials Needed

fondant
*(yellow, black, white
& mustard yellow)*

raw spaghetti

white shimmer
dust & brush

1 yellow stamen

white soft gel paste

toothpick

Cutters Needed

2¼-inch scalloped
circle cutter

round tips
#7 & #10

teardrop cutter

Tools Needed

rolling pin with ⅛-inch
& 1/16-inch guide rings

rolling pastry cutter

knife tool

precision knife

food scissors

honeycomb
embossing mat

Sweet Tips

SIMPLIFY	Make little worker bees instead of a queen bee to decorate the hive. Or omit the bee altogether.
ACCENTUATE	Make small worker bees to decorate additional toppers and hives.
PERSONALIZE	Dip a toothpick into black soft gel to create a bee path on the fondant in the shape of an initial or age and embellish it with a small bee.
EXPAND	Follow the tutorial to make a bear from the Lions, Tigers & Bears collection (p. 76) to add to the hives and honeycombs.
DECORATE & DISPLAY	Utilize honey jars and dippers, pots, and rustic elements to decorate your table. Place your cupcakes in individual tins filled with crushed graham crackers or Honeycomb cereal.

Bee & Hive

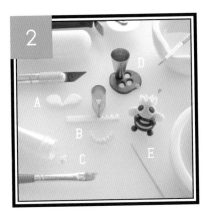

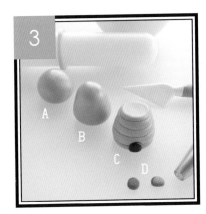

How to:

1. Roll yellow fondant into a ball (approximately ⅔ inch) and narrow the top a bit to create the bee's body. Insert a small piece of raw spaghetti into the center, allowing enough to stick out to support the head. With the rolling pin, roll out black fondant ¹⁄₁₆ inch thick and, with the rolling pastry cutter, cut 3 thin strips to glue around the bee's body **(A)**. Roll another piece of yellow fondant into a ball (approximately ½ inch) to form the head. Use the food scissors to cut the yellow stamen in half and insert both in the bee's head to create antennae. Use round tip #10 at a 45-degree angle to make an indent in the head for the bee's mouth. Roll out white and black fondant ⅛ inch thick and cut out 2 white circles with round tip #10 and 2 black circles with round tip #7. Use your fingers to pinch them a bit, creating ovals **(B)**. Glue them to the bee's head. Glue the head to the body.

2. With the rolling pin, roll out white fondant ⅛ inch thick. Cut out 2 teardrop shapes. Pinch the 2 pointed tips and allow to dry a bit, creating the bee's wings **(A)**. Using the rolling pastry cutter, cut out a strip of the white fondant (approximately ¼ inch wide) and use the pointed tip of the teardrop cutter to remove small triangular sections of the fondant. Turn it up on its side with the pointed tips facing up and bring the ends together to create the crown **(B)**. Mold the crown around the bee's head and cut off any excess with the precision knife. Brush white shimmer dust on both the wings and the crown **(C)** and glue them onto the bee. With the rolling pin, roll out black fondant ⅛ inch thick and cut out 4 circles with round tip #10 **(D)**. Roll them into balls and glue them to the front of the bee to create the limbs. Dip the toothpick into some white soft gel paste and dab it onto the bee's eyes **(E)**.

(continued on next page)

3. Roll the mustard yellow fondant into a ball (approximately 1 inch) **(A)** and narrow the top with your fingers **(B)**. With the knife tool, indent several lines all around the fondant to create the hive **(C)**. Use your fingers to smooth it out once all lines have been made. With the rolling pin, roll out black fondant ⅛ inch thick and use round tip #10 to cut out a circle. Flatten it out with your finger and use the knife tool to shape the bottom into a straight line **(D)**. Glue this to the base of the hive for the entrance. With the rolling pin, roll out yellow fondant ⅛ inch thick and spread shortening over it. Place the honeycomb embossing mat over it and use the rolling pin to impress the pattern on the fondant. Use the 2¼-inch scalloped cutter to punch out a circle and glue the hive to the bottom topper and the queen bee to the top of the hive. Allow to dry thoroughly.

STEP RIGHT UP

fondant
(white, light gray, black, red, yellow, blue & light brown)

raw spaghetti

tylose powder

Cutters Needed

1½-inch circle cutter

1¼-inch & 2¼-inch scalloped circle cutters

round tips
#5, #10 & #12

medium teardrop cutter

various-sized flower cutters

small star cutter

Tools Needed

rolling pin with ⅛-inch & 1/16-inch guide rings

2 wooden dowels

rolling pastry cutter

knife tool

precision knife

small modeling stick

miniature ball tool

fondant storage board

foam block

Sweet Tips

SIMPLIFY	If the three-dimensional figures are too daunting, try making two-dimensional animal faces.
ACCENTUATE	Make extra and larger peanuts to decorate additional cupcakes. Cut out additional flowers, stars, and circles in primary colors to place on colored fondant.
PERSONALIZE	Follow the balloon tutorial from the Piece of Cake collection (p. 21) to add more dimension to cupcakes and personalize them by adding ages or initials.
EXPAND	Add more circus animals with the tutorials from the Lions, Tigers & Bears collection (p. 73) and enhance them with colorful circus accessories.
DECORATE & DISPLAY	Decorate with colorful accessories, real peanuts, and carnival tickets.

Circus Elephant

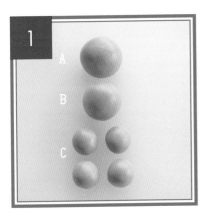

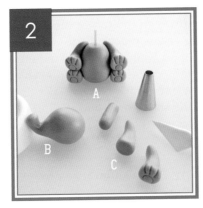

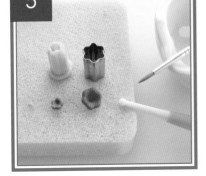

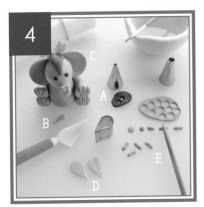

How to:

1. Knead tylose powder into the light gray fondant and roll it into balls as follows: body, 1½-inch (**A**); head, 1¼-inch (**B**); and 4 limbs, ¾-inch (**C**).

2. Form the body into an oval shape and place it on your work surface. Insert a raw spaghetti with enough protruding to hold the head (**A**). Narrow one side of the head to create the trunk. Fold the trunk to the desired direction and set it aside to harden. Lean it up against an object to ensure it keeps its shape (**B**). Make sure to fit the head through the spaghetti before it begins to dry. You can use the small modeling stick to make a hole at the tip of the trunk. Roll out the limbs, keeping one end thick and proportionally narrowing the rest of the arms and legs, forming them around the elephant's body. Flatten the elephant's feet and, with the knife tool, indent the top in 3 places. Use round tip #10 to indent a circle on the bottom (**C**). Glue the limbs to the elephant's body.

3. Glue the elephant's head to the body. With the rolling pin, roll out light gray fondant ⅛ inch thick and, using the 1½-inch cutter, cut out 2 circles (**A**). Allow them to dry a minute, and then shape them to the back of the elephant's head and glue them in place (**B**).

(continued on next page)

4. With the rolling pin, roll out black fondant ⅛ inch thick and use round tip #5 to cut out 2 circles for the eyes **(A)**. Glue the eyes to the elephant's head. Roll out a small piece of light gray fondant, shape it into a small tail **(B)**, and glue it to the elephant's back. With the rolling pin, roll out yellow, red, and blue fondant ⅛ inch thick. Using the medium teardrop cutter, cut out 1 red, 1 blue, and 2 yellow shapes. Dip your finger in shortening and flatten out the blue teardrop. Layer the red teardrop over the blue and glue them to the top of the elephant's head **(C)**. Use the narrow point of the teardrop cutter to trim the yellow pieces diagonally, creating a feather effect. Use the knife tool to make a vertical indentation as well as diagonal indentations to the feathers **(D)**. Glue them to the back of the elephant's head. With the rolling pin, roll out the light brown fondant ⅛ inch thick and use round tip #12 to cut out several circles. Take one and roll it into a ball and then roll it out on your work surface. Using the small modeling stick, roll the center of the light brown fondant to shape it into a peanut and then use the tip to make marks like a peanut shell **(E)**. Repeat for as many peanuts as you wish and glue a couple to the tip of the elephant's trunk.

5. Roll out fondant in different colors and cut flowers with the various-sized cutters. Place them on the foam block and use the miniature ball tool to indent the centers of the flowers, and glue them together. Roll a very small ball of fondant and put in the indentation of the flower. Glue the flower to the elephant. Glue the elephant to the striped topper (p. 72). Allow to dry thoroughly.

Circus Seal

LEVEL OF DIFFICULTY

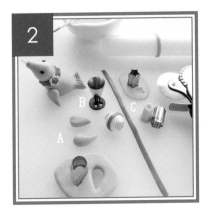

How to:

1. Knead tylose powder into the light gray fondant and roll it into a ¾-inch ball and a 1¼-inch ball. Shape the smaller ball into the seal's head by narrowing one side to create the nose (45- to 90-degree angle) **(A)**. Dip your fingers in shortening and shape the larger ball into an oval. Begin pulling one side of the bottom out to create the seal's tail, but ensure the body is still sitting up. Flatten the tail a bit with your finger and use the knife tool or precision knife to indent the center of the tail and make marks on the sides. Insert a raw spaghetti into the body, but make sure it is long enough to go all the way through the head and into the ball **(B)**. Use another raw spaghetti to carefully make a hole from the bottom of the head through the tip of the nose. Once the two pieces have hardened enough, glue the head to the body. With the rolling pin, roll out red fondant ⅛ inch thick and use the 1¼-inch scalloped cutter to punch out a circle. Use the bottom of one of the round tips to cut out the center of the scalloped circle. Use the precision knife to cut through one side and shape it around the seal, trimming the excess. Glue the collar to the seal **(C)**. (Tip: The more vertical you shape the seal's body and its head, the less chance it has to tip over when put together. Be cognizant of the weight distribution, including the ball to be placed on its nose later.)

2. Roll out light gray fondant thick with the rolling pin and wooden dowels. Use the teardrop cutter to punch out 2 shapes and use shortening to round them out and shape them into the seal's flippers **(A)**. Shape them to the sides of the seal and glue them on. With the rolling pin, roll out black fondant ⅛ inch thick and use round tip #5 to cut out the eyes **(B)**. Glue them to the seal's head. For the seal's ball, roll a piece of white fondant into a ball and set aside to dry a bit. Change out the guide rings on the rolling pin and roll out blue and yellow fondant ¹⁄₁₆ inch thick. Use the rolling pastry cutter to cut a strip of blue fondant and glue around the center of the ball. Cut 2 stars out of the yellow fondant and glue them to opposite sides of the ball **(C)**. When the ball is hardened enough to keep its shape, insert it through the protruding raw spaghetti and glue it to the seal's nose. Replicate the flowers from the circus elephant tutorial (p. 70) and glue them to the seal's collar. Glue the seal to the striped topper (p. 72). Allow to dry thoroughly.

Striped Topper

How to:

1. With the rolling pin, roll out red and white fondant ⅛ inch thick. Use the rolling pastry cutter to cut out strips approximately ¼ inch wide. Place them inside the fondant storage board to avoid drying out. Switch out the guide rings on the rolling pin to ¹⁄₁₆ inch and roll out white fondant. Spread glue onto the thin fondant and start placing the red and white stripes across. Once the pattern is complete, utilize the 2¼-inch scalloped cutter to punch out a circle for the bottom of the toppers. Glue the circus animals to the striped toppers. Allow to dry thoroughly.

LIONS, TIGERS & BEARS

Materials Needed

fondant
(brown, dark brown, black, tan, ivory & orange)

raw spaghetti

tylose powder

Cutters Needed

1⅞-inch & 2¼-inch
scalloped circle cutters

round tips
#7 & #12

small oval cutter

small teardrop cutter

Tools Needed

rolling pin with
⅛-inch guide rings

2 wooden dowels

knife tool

precision knife

modeling tool

small modeling stick

2 flower-forming cups

Sweet Tips

SIMPLIFY	Follow the instructions to make the jungle animal faces, but rather than a ball, simply roll out fondant flat and cut out with a round shape.
ACCENTUATE	Use different-sized leaf cutters to punch out jungle leaves to easily embellish additional cupcakes.
PERSONALIZE	Punch initials or ages out of fondant and add them to fondant leaves or roll out fondant to resemble snakes and shape them into letters and/or numbers.
EXPAND	Follow the horse tutorial from the Down on the Farm collection (p. 55), paired with the stripes instructions from the tiger tutorial, to create a zebra. Follow the tutorial for the circus elephant from the Step Right Up collection (p. 69) for a jungle elephant. Follow the tutorial for the monkey from the Monkeying Around collection (p. 81) to add to the jungle figures.
DECORATE & DISPLAY	Use burlap and leaves to match the jungle theme and add green frosting to the cupcakes.

Animal Body

LEVEL OF DIFFICULTY

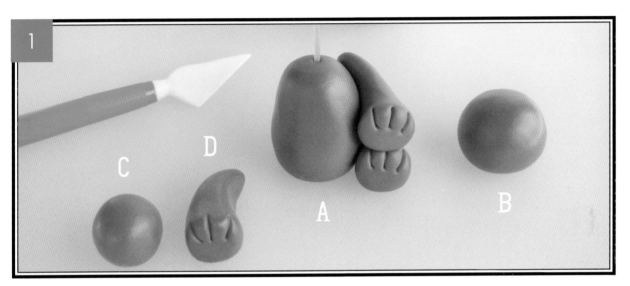

How to:

1. Knead tylose powder into (brown, tan, or orange) fondant and roll it into balls as follows: body, 1¼-inch **(A)**; head, 1-inch **(B)**; 4 limbs, ¾-inch **(C)**. Roll the body into an oval shape, narrowed a little at the top. Insert a piece of raw spaghetti by twisting it through the center, leaving enough protruding to hold up the head. Roll out the limbs, keeping one end thick and proportionally narrowing the rest of the arms and legs, forming them around the body. Use the knife tool to make three indentations at the top of the paws **(D)**. Glue the limbs to the body. Insert the head over the body and raw spaghetti to mold it to fit, but allow it and the body to dry longer on your work surface prior to gluing. (**Please note**: If you are making the lion, follow the instructions for the mane prior to gluing the head to the body.

Bear

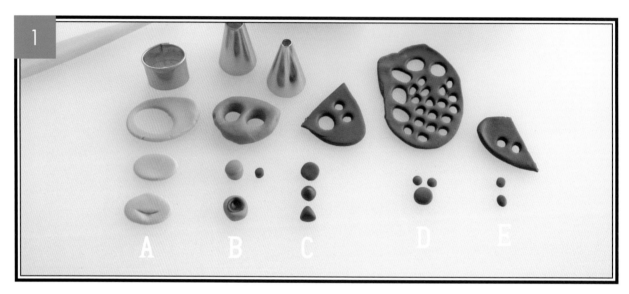

How to:

1. With the rolling pin, roll out tan fondant ⅛ inch thick and cut out a small oval with the cutter. Use the bottom of a round tip to indent a mouth **(A)**. With the rolling pin and wooden dowels, roll out brown fondant thick. Cut out 2 circles with round tip #12. Round them out a bit with your fingers. With the rolling pin, roll out dark brown fondant ⅛ inch thick and cut out 2 circles with round tip #7. Roll them into balls and flatten them out a bit. Glue the smaller dark brown circles to the larger brown ones and indent the center with the modeling tool. Flatten out the bottom to form the ears **(B)**. With the rolling pin, roll out dark brown fondant ⅛ inch thick and cut out a circle with round tip #12. Roll it into a ball and then shape it into a triangle to form the nose **(C)**. With the rolling pin, roll out dark brown fondant ⅛ inch thick. Cut out 4 circles with round tip #12 and 16 circles with round tip #7 for the paws **(D)**. With the rolling pin, roll out black fondant ⅛ inch thick and cut out 2 circles with round tip #7. Shape them into ovals with your fingers to create the eyes **(E)**. Glue all the facial features and paw pads to the bear. Allow to dry thoroughly.

Lion

How to:

1. With the rolling pin, roll out brown fondant ⅛ inch thick. Cut out circles with the 1⅞-inch and 2¼-inch scalloped cutters. Coat the flower-forming cups with a bit of powdered sugar and place the 2 scalloped circles in the cups, leaving a bit protruding out of one side only for the top of the mane **(A)**. With the rolling pin, roll out tan fondant ⅛ inch thick and cut out 2 teardrop shapes with the cutter. Coil the tips upward and join them together. Use the small modeling stick to indent 3 circles for the whiskers **(B)**. With the rolling pin, roll out dark brown fondant ⅛ inch thick and cut out a circle with round tip #12. Roll it into a ball and then form it into a triangle to make the nose **(C)**. With the rolling pin, roll out black fondant ⅛ inch thick and cut out 2 circles with round tip #7. Form them into ovals with your fingers to create the eyes **(D)**. With the rolling pin and wooden dowels, roll out tan fondant thick. Cut out 2 circles with round tip #12. Round them out with your fingers and use the modeling tool to indent the center. Flatten the bottoms to create the ears **(E)**. With the rolling pin, roll out brown fondant ⅛ inch thick. Cut out 4 circles with round tip #12 and 16 circles with round tip #7 for the paws **(F)**. Once the circles for the mane are dry enough to hold their shapes but are still a bit malleable, glue them to the lion's head and insert and glue the head over the body. Glue all the facial features and paw pads to the lion as well. Allow to dry thoroughly.

Tiger

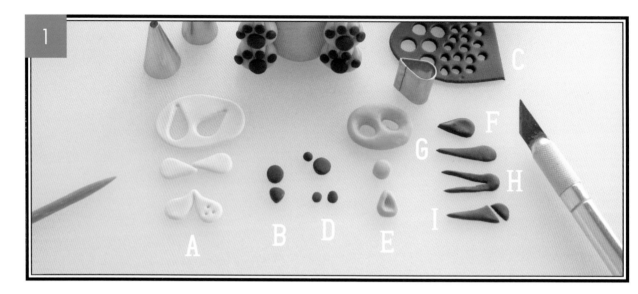

How to:

1. With the rolling pin, roll out ivory fondant ⅛ inch thick and cut out 2 small teardrop shapes with the cutter. Coil the tips upward and join them together. Use the small modeling stick to indent 3 circles for the whiskers (**A**). With the rolling pin, roll out black fondant ⅛ inch thick. Cut out 5 circles with round tip #12 and 18 circles with round tip #7. Take one of the bigger circles, ball it up, and form it into a triangle to form the nose (**B**). The 4 large circles and 16 of the smaller circles will serve as the paw pads (**C**). Shape the remaining 2 small circles into ovals to form the eyes (**D**). With the rolling pin and wooden dowels, roll out orange fondant thick and cut out 2 circles with round tip #12. Use the modeling tool to indent the centers and shape them into triangles to form the ears (**E**). With the rolling pin, roll out black fondant ⅛ inch thick, spread shortening over it, and cut out several small teardrop shapes with the cutter (**F**). You can use different techniques to create the tiger stripes: Elongate the teardrop shapes with your fingers (**G**) and glue the long, narrow strips on the front and the wider end on the back of the tiger, as I did at the top of the tiger's head. And/or you can elongate the teardrop shape and cut a slit through the center with the precision knife (**H**), as I did with the stripes on the side of the tiger's face. And/or you can elongate the teardrop shape and cut off the excess of the wider end with the precision knife (**I**), as I did with the stripes on the tiger's limbs. Glue all the facial features, stripes, and paw pads to the tiger. Allow to dry thoroughly.

MONKEYING AROUND

Materials Needed

fondant
(brown, ivory & black)

raw spaghetti

tylose powder

Cutters Needed

round tips
#7 & #12

medium heart cutter

small oval cutter

Tools Needed

rolling pin with
⅛-inch guide rings

2 wooden dowels

knife tool

precision knife

modeling tool

Sweet Tips

SIMPLIFY	To make a flat monkey topper, follow the instructions to make the monkey face, but rather than a ball, simply roll out fondant flat and cut out with a round shape.
ACCENTUATE	Add jungle leaves and bananas to additional cupcakes.
PERSONALIZE	Make more monkey tails or tree vines with small leaves and shape them into initials and ages.
EXPAND	Add the monkey to the Lions, Tigers & Bears collection (p. 73) to create a large jungle animal presentation.
DECORATE & DISPLAY	Decorate with jungle leaves, real bananas, and yellow cupcake liners.

Monkey

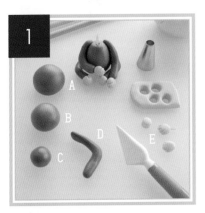

How to:

1. Knead tylose powder into brown fondant and roll it into balls as follows: body 1-inch **(A)**; head, ⅞-inch **(B)**; 4 limbs, ½-inch **(C)**. Roll the body into an oval shape, narrowed a little at the top. Insert a piece of raw spaghetti into the top of the body by twisting it through the center, leaving enough protruding to hold up the head. Roll out the limbs, bending at the elbows and knees, loosely forming them around the body **(D)**. With the rolling pin and wooden dowels, roll out ivory fondant thick and cut out 4 circles with round tip #12. Roll them into balls and then use the knife tool to indent fingers and toes accordingly. Insert a small piece of raw spaghetti into the hands so they will attach securely to the arms **(E)**. Glue the hands and feet to the limbs.

2. With the rolling pin, roll out ivory fondant ⅛ inch thick and cut out a heart, a small oval, and a #7 circle with the respective cutters. Trim off the bottom of the heart with the precision knife **(A)**. Roll the oval into a ball, and then shape the ball into an oval. Use round tip #12 at a 45-degree angle to indent the mouth in the side of the oval **(B)**. Roll the small circle into an oval for the nose **(C)**. With the rolling pin, roll out black fondant ⅛ inch thick and cut out 2 circles with round tip #7 for the eyes **(D)**. Glue all the facial features to the monkey's head. With the rolling pin, roll brown fondant ⅛ inch thick and cut out 3 ovals with the cutter. Roll 2 of the ovals into balls and indent the centers with the modeling tool. With the rolling pin, roll out ivory fondant ⅛ inch thick and cut out 2 circles with round tip #12. Glue them to the indented center of the brown circles and smooth it out with the modeling tool. Pinch the ends together and flatten to fit on the sides of the monkey's head for the ears **(E)**. Glue on the ears. Roll the remaining small brown oval into a ball and then roll it out onto your work surface. Coil the end of the strip with your fingers to form the tail **(F)**. Glue the tail to the back of the monkey with the coil peeking out to the side. Glue all the parts together and allow to dry thoroughly.

"X" MARKS THE SPOT

Materials Needed

fondant
*(light brown, dark brown,
black, red, yellow, blue,
ivory & white)*

white, black & brown
soft gel paste

toothpick

raw spaghetti

tylose powder

Cutters Needed

1¼-inch, 1½-inch &
2¼-inch circle cutters

round tips
#2, #3, #7,
#10 & #12

Tools Needed

rolling pin with
⅛-inch guide rings

2 wooden dowels

rolling pastry cutter

knife tool

precision knife

small modeling stick

Sweet Tips

SIMPLIFY	Make a two-dimensional pirate face with the same features. Simply draw on the elements on the treasure map. Omit the waves or the sail from the pirate ship.
ACCENTUATE	Punch out bigger circles and paint them with gold shimmer to create gold coins for additional cupcakes.
PERSONALIZE	Punch out initials or ages and glue them to fondant gold coins.
EXPAND	Follow the tutorial for the striped topper from the Step Right Up collection (p. 72) to add to the pirate assortment.
DECORATE & DISPLAY	Enhance your display with eye patches and plastic or chocolate gold coins. Use cupcake liners with pirate paraphernalia and display the cupcakes in individual low-cost salsa bowls.

Pirate Ship

LEVEL OF DIFFICULTY

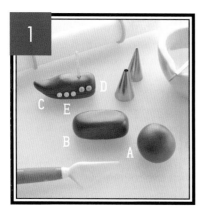

How to:

1. Roll light brown fondant into a ball (approximately 1 inch) **(A)** and shape it into a long rectangular cube **(B)**. With your fingers dipped in shortening, shape the rectangle into the ship, narrowing one end and pulling the tip upward, and flattening the other end. Use the knife tool to make a large indent on the bottom third of the ship and to make smaller marks around the vessel **(C)**. With the rolling pin, roll out yellow fondant ⅛ inch thick and cut out 2 circles with round tip #7. Use the knife tool to make 2 crossing lines and glue the windows to the ship **(D)**. With the rolling pin, roll out white fondant ⅛ inch thick and cut out 3 circles with round tip #7. Glue the circles to the ship and use round tip #3 to indent the center of the portholes **(E)**. Insert a raw spaghetti into the ship to hold the sail.

2. With the rolling pin, roll out red fondant ⅛ inch thick and cut out a rectangle 2 × 1½ inches with the rolling pastry cutter **(A)**. Turn it upside down and roll both sides into each other **(B)**. Turn it back around and ensure the sail is not flat but puffed out a bit. Roll a bit of light brown fondant on your work surface and insert the raw spaghetti from the ship into the brown fondant. Roll it over the surface to even and smooth it out and use the precision knife to cut off the excess, making sure there is enough spaghetti exposed to insert back into the ship **(C)**. With the rolling pin, roll out black fondant ⅛ inch thick and use the precision knife to cut out a small rectangle **(D)**. Cut out a small piece from one end to create the flag and pinch the points a bit to shape them upward **(E)**. Glue the sail and the flag to the pole and allow it to dry a bit **(F)**. Take various sizes of blue fondant and roll them into balls. Roll the balls out on the surface with your fingers and start rolling them into themselves to create waves **(G)**. With the rolling pin, roll out blue fondant ⅛ inch thick and use the 2¼-inch cutter to cut out the bottom topper. Glue the rolling waves to the bottom topper, using the ship as a guide **(H)**. When the sail is dry enough and secured to the pole, insert and glue the pole into the ship and glue the ship to the bottom topper, with the waves in front. Allow to dry thoroughly.

Treasure Map

LEVEL OF DIFFICULTY

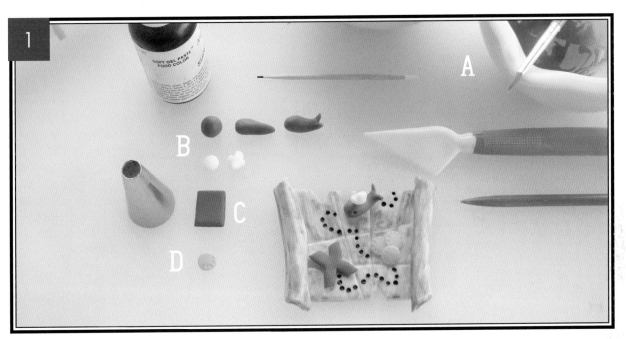

How to:

1. With the rolling pin, roll out ivory fondant ⅛ inch thick and cut out a rectangle 3 × 2 inches. Pull all 4 corners a bit with your fingers. Roll the 2 narrow sides up and into the map, narrowing the bottom a bit more. Use the knife tool to create linear indentations on the map. Use the brown soft gel paste mixed with water to brush on some color to the map to age it. Make sure the paste is watered down so it doesn't turn out too dark. You can always use your brush dipped in water to clean it up more, if necessary (A). To make the whale, roll blue fondant into a ball (approximately ¼ inch) and shape it into a teardrop. Use the knife to cut a slit at the narrow end and shape it upward to create the whale's tail. Use the small modeling stick to indent eyes. With the rolling pin, roll out white fondant ⅛ inch thick and cut out a circle with round tip #12. Shape it into a teardrop and use the knife tool to indent it twice on the wider end to create the water coming out of the spout (B). Glue it to the top of the whale. With the rolling pin, roll red fondant ⅛ inch thick and cut out a small rectangle (C). Use the precision knife to cut out an "X" shape. With the rolling pin, roll out yellow fondant ⅛ inch thick and cut out 3 circles with round tip #12. Make indentations around the circles for added details on the gold coins (D). Place and glue all pieces to the map and use the small modeling stick to make dots for the path on the map. Dip a toothpick in black soft gel paste and insert it in the dots. Allow to dry thoroughly.

TO THE RESCUE

Materials Needed

fondant
*(red, yellow, blue,
skin-colored & white)*

black edible-ink
marker

Cutters Needed

1⅞-inch & 2¼-inch
circle cutters

round tip #2

large teardrop cutter

small hand cutter

small star cutter

letter cutters
(A, B, M, P, W & Z)

Tools Needed

rolling pin with ⅛-inch
& 1/16-inch guide rings

modeling tool

small modeling stick

rolling pastry cutter

dotted embossing mat

Sweet Tips

SIMPLIFY	Omit the shirt and hands and replace with a bigger star.
ACCENTUATE	Cut out a variety of sizes of stars to accentuate additional cupcakes. Cut them out thick and add them to lollipop sticks so they stand up in your cupcakes.
PERSONALIZE	Instead of a star on the superhero shirt, add an age or initial. Add initials, ages, or names (if short enough) inside the word bubbles or simply write them out with the edible-ink marker.
EXPAND	Follow the tutorial from the Red, White & Boom collection (p. 188) to make fireworks with matching colors.
DECORATE & DISPLAY	Find superhero supplies, such as masks, to enhance your presentation. Make buildings out of building blocks or cardboard boxes for a background.

Shirt Reveal

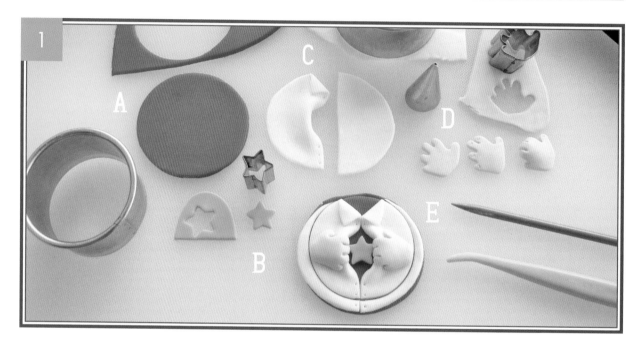

How to:

1. With the rolling pin, roll out red fondant ⅛ inch thick and cut out a 2¼-inch circle with the cutter (**A**). Roll out yellow fondant with the rolling pin ⅛ inch thick and cut out a small star with the cutter (**B**). Glue the star to the center of the red circle. With the rolling pin, roll out white fondant 1/16 inch thick and cut out a 2¼-inch circle with the cutter. Use the rolling pastry cutter to cut the circle in half. Fold over the top end of both sides to create the shirt collars. Pick up 1 semicircle and start to push the straight side over in the center with your finger, tucking it underneath. Place it back onto your work surface and use the modeling tool to push it farther inward. Repeat with the other semicircle. Use the small modeling stick to indent little buttons on the shirt (**C**). Fit the shirt over the red circle and adjust the opening enough to reveal the star. With the rolling pin, roll out skin-colored fondant ⅛ inch thick and cut out 2 hands with the small cutter. Make sure to cut 1 hand out and then turn the fondant upside down to cut the second hand so that the hands are in opposite directions. (If you do not have a hand cutter, cut out an oval and use a precision knife to cut out the fingers, round them, and shape into a hand.) Use round tip #2 to indent fingernails on the ends of the fingers and round out the hand with the fingers tucking underneath (**D**). Place the hands over the sides of the shirt that are opened and mold them to fit. Glue the shirt and hands on the red circle and use the 1⅞-inch circle cutter to trim the circle to size (**E**). Use the edible-ink marker to draw buttons onto the shirt. Allow to dry thoroughly.

Superhero Sounds

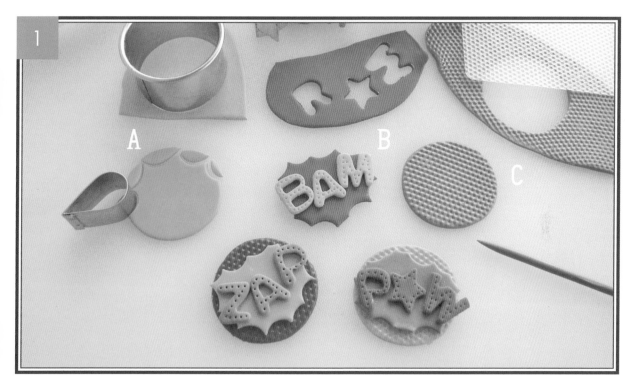

How to:

1. With the rolling pin, roll out colored fondant ⅛ inch thick. Cut out a 1⅞-inch circle with the cutter. Use the wider end of the large teardrop cutter to cut around the perimeter of the circle, turning the cutter in different angles as you move around the circle to create the word bubbles (**A**). With the rolling pin, roll out colored fondant ⅛ inch thick and use the letter cutters to punch out the sayings. Use the small modeling stick to indent dots in the middle of the letters. Glue the letters to the previously cut word bubbles (**B**). With the rolling pin, roll out colored fondant ⅛ inch thick and spread a bit of shortening over the fondant. Place the dotted embossing mat over the fondant and use the rolling pin to impress the pattern onto it. Use the 1⅞-inch cutter to punch out a circle (**C**). Glue the word bubble to the circles. Repeat for the other word bubbles. Allow to dry thoroughly. When dry, use a black edible-ink marker to outline the word bubbles.

UNDER CONSTRUCTION

Materials Needed

fondant
(yellow, orange, light gray, black & white)

Cutters Needed

1¼-inch, 1⅞-inch & 2¼-inch circle cutters

round tips
#1, #7, #10 & #12

large square cutter

small circle cutter

small & medium oval cutters

Tools Needed

rolling pin with ⅛-inch & 1⁄16-inch guide rings

2 wooden dowels

knife tool

precision knife

small modeling stick

large ball tool

dotted embossing mat

Sweet Tips

SIMPLIFY	Omit the construction hat. Or separate the hat and cone on different toppers.
ACCENTUATE	Make the construction hat and cone larger to fit them on separate cupcakes if you want to spread them out.
PERSONALIZE	Roll out a long piece of orange fondant to resemble an electric cord and shape it into an initial or age. Add a small square to the end for the plug.
EXPAND	Follow the tutorial to make tires from the Start Your Engines collection (p. 146) to embellish additional cupcakes.
DECORATE & DISPLAY	Adorn your display with galvanized buckets, hard hats, real cones, and toy construction trucks. To resemble dirt, add crushed Oreo cookies to your frosting and serving ware.

Hat & Cone

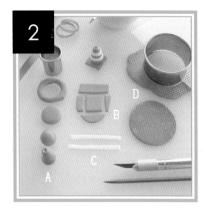

How to:

1. With the rolling pin and wooden dowels, roll out yellow fondant thick and cut out a 1⅞-inch circle with the cutter. Roll it into a ball (**A**) and use the knife tool to make 4 indentations at the top of the hat. With the rolling pin, roll out more yellow fondant ⅛ inch thick and cut out a medium oval with the cutter. To form the brim, flatten and square out the bottom a little and use the circle cutter to trim off the top (**B**). Smooth it out and glue the top to the brim. With the rolling pin, roll out yellow fondant ⅛ inch thick and use the large square cutter and precision knife to trim 3 small rectangles. Glue 1 vertically to the front and the remaining 2 horizontally to each side of the hat. Cut out a circle with round tip #10 and glue it over the strip on the front of the hat (**C**).

2. With the rolling pin and wooden dowels, roll out orange fondant thick and cut out a circle with the 1¼-inch cutter. Roll the circle into a ball and then shape it into a cone. Use the small modeling stick to make a hole at the top of the cone (**A**). With the rolling pin, roll out orange fondant ⅛ inch thick and use the large square cutter to trim a square to fit under the cone (**B**). Glue the cone to the square base. With the rolling pin, roll out white fondant ⅛ inch thick and use the large square cutter to cut 2 long strips (**C**). Fit them around the cone, trim them, and glue them in place. With the rolling pin, roll out light gray fondant ⅛ inch thick and spread a bit of shortening over the fondant. Place the embossing mat over the fondant and use the rolling pin to impress the pattern onto it. Use the 2¼-inch cutter to punch out a circle (**D**) and glue the hat and cone to it. Allow to dry thoroughly.

Construction Truck

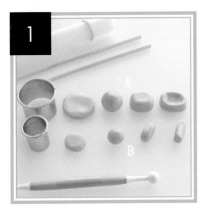

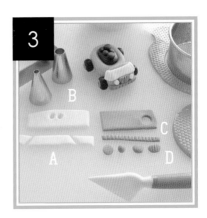

How to:

1. With the rolling pin and wooden dowels, roll out yellow fondant thick. Cut out a 1¼-inch circle and a 1⅞-inch circle. Roll the larger circle into a ball and then form it into a rectangular cube. Use the knife tool to indent the truck markings around the truck bed. Use the large ball tool to hollow out the center **(A)**. Roll the smaller circle into a ball, and then form it into a rectangular cube on its side. Use your fingers dipped in shortening to shape the windshield area, making a diagonal slant on the top portion **(B)**.

2. With the rolling pin, roll out yellow fondant ⅛ inch thick and cut out a large square with the cutter. Trim into a rectangle **(A)** to fit underneath the cab and bed of the truck, and then glue them together. With the rolling pin and wooden dowels, roll out black fondant thick and cut out a small oval with the cutter. With your fingers dipped in shortening, round out the sides and shape it to fit in the hollowed-out truck bed **(B)**. With the rolling pin, roll out black fondant ⅛ inch thick. Cut out 4 circles with the small cutter, roll them into balls, and then shape them into tires. With the rolling pin, roll out orange fondant ⅛ inch thick and cut out 4 circles with round tip #7. Glue them to the center of the tires and use round tip #1 to indent the centers. Use the corner of the large square cutter to make indentations around the tire for treads **(C)**. Glue the four tires to the truck. With the leftover rolled-out black fondant, cut out a few circles with round tips #7 and #10, roll them into uneven balls, and glue them to the top of the truck bed **(D)**.

3. With the rolling pin, roll out white fondant ⅛ inch thick and use the large square cutter to cut out a strip to make the windshield **(A)**. Fit it over the front of the truck, trim it, and glue it to the truck. Cut 2 circles out of the white fondant with round tip #7 for the headlights **(B)** and glue them to the truck. With the rolling pin, roll out light gray fondant ⅛ inch thick and cut a thin strip with the large

(continued on next page)

(continued):

square cutter. Use the knife tool to indent it all the way across **(C)**, trim it, and glue it on the truck as the front fender. With the light gray fondant, cut out 1 circle with round tip #12, roll it into a ball, and then flatten it out while narrowing one end. Use the knife tool to indent the grill **(D)** and glue it to the front of the truck. With the rolling pin, roll out orange fondant ⅛ inch thick and spread a bit of shortening over the fondant. Place the embossing mat over the fondant and use the rolling pin to impress the pattern onto it. Use the 2¼-inch circle cutter to punch out a circle and glue the truck to it. Allow to dry thoroughly.

SOUND THE ALARM

Materials Needed

fondant
*(yellow, red, light gray,
light brown & white)*

Cutters Needed

$\frac{7}{8}$-inch, $1\frac{7}{8}$-inch &
$2\frac{1}{4}$-inch circle cutters

round tips
#2 & #12

large square cutter

small circle cutter

Tools Needed

rolling pin with
$\frac{1}{8}$-inch guide rings

2 wooden dowels

knife tool

precision knife

large modeling stick

brick pattern
embossing mat

Sweet Tips

SIMPLIFY	Omit the ax and center the hose on the topper and/or remove the shield from the helmet.
ACCENTUATE	Use different-sized teardrop cutters to cut flames out of red and yellow fondant to accentuate additional cupcakes.
PERSONALIZE	Make a larger hose and shape it into an age or an initial on another cupcake.
EXPAND	Follow the tutorial for fireworks from the Red, White & Boom collection (p. 188), but replace the stars with teardrop shapes for flames in the appropriate colors.
DECORATE & DISPLAY	Bake your cupcakes in red liners and decorate with yellow frosting to match. Embellish your presentation with toy fire trucks or related decorations.

Fire Helmet

LEVEL OF DIFFICULTY

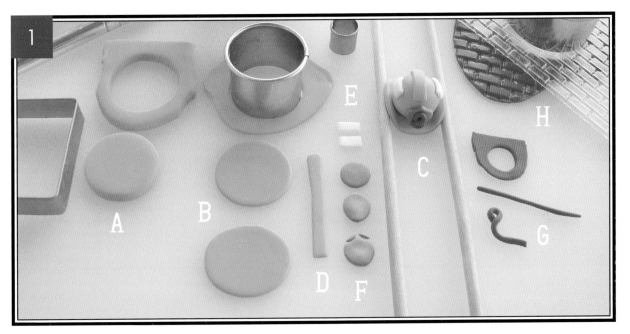

How to:

1. With the rolling pin and wooden dowels, roll out yellow fondant thick and cut out a circle with the 1⅞-inch cutter **(A)**. Roll it into a ball to form the top of the helmet. With the rolling pin, roll out yellow fondant ⅛ inch thick and cut out a circle with the 1⅞-inch cutter. Pull the sides out lightly with your finger to widen the brim a little **(B)**. Place the brim between 2 wooden dowels with the sides propped up and glue the top of the helmet to it **(C)**. With the rolling pin, roll out yellow fondant ⅛ inch thick and cut out a strip with the large square cutter **(D)**. Fit it over the top of the helmet, trim it, and glue it in place. With the rolling pin, roll out white fondant ⅛ inch thick and use the precision knife to cut out 2 small rectangles **(E)**. Glue them horizontally to each side of the helmet. With the rolling pin, roll out light gray fondant ⅛ inch thick and cut out a small circle with the cutter. Shape the bottom into a tip as a wide teardrop shape and use the small circle cutter to trim the top into a point to resemble a shield **(F)**. Glue it to the front of the helmet. Roll out red fondant on the work surface and shape it to the desired number or letter **(G)** and glue it to the shield. With the rolling pin, roll out red fondant ⅛ inch thick and spread a bit of shortening over the fondant. Place the embossing mat over the fondant and use the rolling pin to impress the pattern onto it. Use the 2¼-inch cutter to punch out a circle **(H)**. Glue the helmet to the base. Allow to dry thoroughly.

Fire Hose & Ax

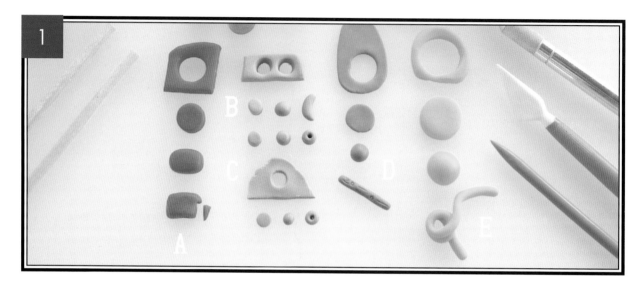

How to:

1. Roll out red fondant thick with the rolling pin and wooden dowels. Cut out a small circle with the cutter and shape it into a rounded rectangle. With the precision knife, trim off a piece of one end, leaving a small tip at the top. Shape the opposite end with a diagonal slant. Use the large modeling stick to make a hole at the bottom of the ax where the handle will be inserted **(A)**. Roll out light gray fondant thick with the rolling pin and wooden dowels. Cut out 2 circles with round tip #12. Roll 1 circle into a ball and then form it into a crescent shape. Fit it and glue it over the red diagonal part of the axe. Roll the second circle into a cylindrical shape, use the knife tool to indent the perimeter of it, and use the large modeling stick to make a hole at the opening of the hose nozzle **(B)**. With the rolling pin, roll the light gray fondant $\frac{1}{8}$ inch thick and use round tip #12 to cut out a circle. Roll it into a ball, flatten it, and use round tip #2 to indent the center for the other side of the hose **(C)**. With the rolling pin, roll out light brown fondant $\frac{1}{8}$ inch thick, cut out a small circle with the cutter, and roll it into a ball. Then roll it out on your work surface to form the axe handle. Use round tip #2 to indent a couple of wood circles and use the knife tool to indent wood grain lines **(D)**. Allow it to dry enough to keep its shape and insert it and glue it into the bottom of the ax. With the rolling pin and wooden dowels, roll out yellow fondant thick and cut out a $\frac{7}{8}$-inch circle with the cutter. Roll it into a ball and then roll it out long. Shape it into a fire hose by coiling it a bit in the center, leaving the ends accessible **(E)**. Glue the 2 light gray nozzles you previously made to the ends. With the rolling pin, roll out white fondant $\frac{1}{8}$ inch thick and spread a bit of shortening over the fondant. Place the embossing mat over the fondant and use the rolling pin to impress the pattern onto it. Use the $2\frac{1}{4}$-inch cutter to punch out a circle. Glue the hose and axe to the circle. Allow to dry thoroughly.

MAD SCIENCE

Materials Needed

fondant
(green, purple, light gray, white & light peach)

Cutters Needed

$\frac{7}{8}$-inch, 1$\frac{1}{2}$-inch & 2$\frac{1}{4}$-inch circle cutters

round tips
#7 & #12

small circle cutter

Tools Needed

rolling pin with $\frac{1}{8}$-inch guide rings

2 wooden dowels

knife tool

precision knife

small modeling stick

square pattern embossing mat

Sweet Tips

SIMPLIFY	Decrease the number of beakers or the liquid/smoke coming out of them. Make a smaller brain so there is less you have to cover with the zigzag fondant.
ACCENTUATE	Cut white toppers to look like lab coats or pockets. Add more smoke/liquid to additional cupcakes.
PERSONALIZE	Make radioactive signs with initials or ages in the center.
EXPAND	Follow the tutorial for books from the Bookworm collection (p. 157) to make science books.
DECORATE & DISPLAY	Use trays and beakers or vases to accent your presentation. Use dry ice or cotton candy to decorate smoke coming out of jars and beakers.

Science Beakers

LEVEL OF DIFFICULTY

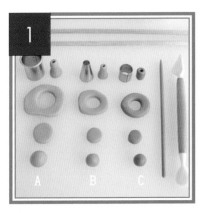

How to:

1. With the rolling pin and wooden dowels, roll out light gray fondant thick and cut out a ⅞-inch circle with the cutter. Roll it into a ball and then with your fingers roll and narrow the top of it like a beaker. Use the knife tool to indent measurement lines and use the small modeling stick to make a hole for the beaker opening (**A**). With the rolling pin and wooden dowels, roll out green fondant thick and use the bottom of a round tip to cut out a circle. Roll it into a ball and then with your fingers roll and narrow the top of it like a beaker. Use the knife tool to indent measurement lines and use the small modeling stick to make a hole for the beaker opening (**B**). With the rolling pin and wooden dowels, roll purple fondant thick and cut out a small circle with the cutter. Roll it into a ball and shape it into a cylinder. Use the knife tool to indent measurement lines and use the small modeling stick to make a hole for the opening (**C**).

2. With the rolling pin, roll out green fondant ⅛ inch thick and use round tip #7 to cut 20–25 circles (**A**). Ball them up and glue them to the top of the light gray beaker coming out of the opening and down the side. Save a few little green balls to embellish the bottom topper at the end. With the rolling pin, roll out purple fondant ⅛ inch thick and cut a small circle with the cutter. Roll it into a ball and then roll it out on your work surface with your fingers, keeping one end thicker (**B**). Insert the narrow end into the green beaker and cascade it down the side with the wider end on the work surface to later glue to the bottom topper. With the rolling pin and wooden dowels, roll out white fondant thick and cut out a circle with round tip #12. Roll it into a ball and then shape it into a teardrop, narrowing out the point to fit into the beaker. Use the knife tool to make 2 indentations at the top of the smoke (**C**). Then insert and glue it into the purple beaker. With the rolling pin, roll out white fondant ⅛ inch thick and cut out a 1½-inch circle with the cutter. With the rolling pin, roll out green fondant ⅛ inch thick and spread a bit of shortening over the fondant. Place the embossing mat over the fondant and use the rolling pin to impress the pattern onto it. Use the 2¼-inch cutter to punch out a circle (**D**). Glue the white circle onto the embossed circle, followed by the beakers. Allow to dry thoroughly.

Brain

LEVEL OF DIFFICULTY

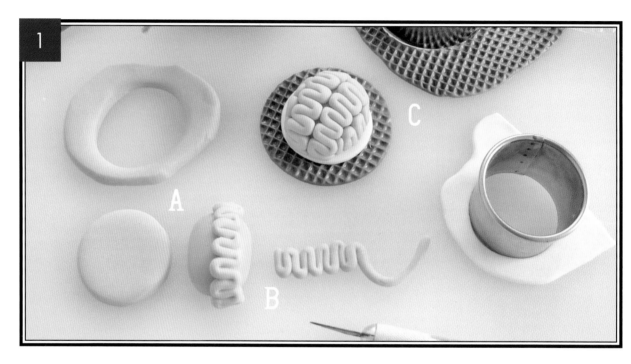

How to:

1. With the rolling pin and wooden dowels, roll out light peach fondant thick and cut out a 1½-inch circle with the cutter. Roll it into a ball, then shape it into an oval, lying flat on your work surface **(A)**. Roll out a long piece of light peach fondant onto your work surface and start shaping into a narrow wave. Fit it lengthwise over the oval with one side touching the center. Glue it and trim the excess with the precision knife **(B)**. Repeat for the other side of the center. Make 2 smaller waves to fit into the remaining sections on each side of the brain and glue them in place. Reshape the brain with your fingers as needed. With the rolling pin, roll out white fondant ⅛ inch thick and cut out a 1½-inch circle with the cutter. With the rolling pin, roll out purple fondant ⅛ inch thick and spread a bit of shortening over the fondant. Place the embossing mat over the fondant and use the rolling pin to impress the pattern onto it. Use the 2¼-inch cutter to punch out a circle. Glue the white circle to the embossed circle, and then glue on the brain **(C)**. Allow to dry thoroughly.

WORK OF ART

Materials Needed

fondant
(white, brown, black, light gray, red, orange, yellow, green & blue)

silver shimmer
dust & brush

Cutters Needed

⅞-inch & 2¼-inch
circle cutters

⅞-inch scalloped
circle cutter

round tip #12

small circle cutter

large leaf cutter

large square cutter

small flower cutter

Tools Needed

rolling pin with ⅛-inch
& ¹⁄₁₆-inch guide rings

2 wooden dowels

precision knife

small modeling stick

Sweet Tips

SIMPLIFY	Omit the paintbrush from the palette and the paint tube and/or crayon from the canvas.
ACCENTUATE	Punch out circles, flowers, and irregular shapes in various colors to make paint splotches to decorate additional cupcakes.
PERSONALIZE	Punch out initials and ages in different colors "painted" on canvases. You can roll out one end/tip and insert it into a paint tube as if it were just painted!
EXPAND	Follow the tutorial to make a chalkboard from the Bookworm collection (p. 157) to add to the art supplies.
DECORATE & DISPLAY	Use actual art palettes, canvas boards, or frames to present your cupcakes. Fill small paint cans with colorful candy for your display.

Paint Palette

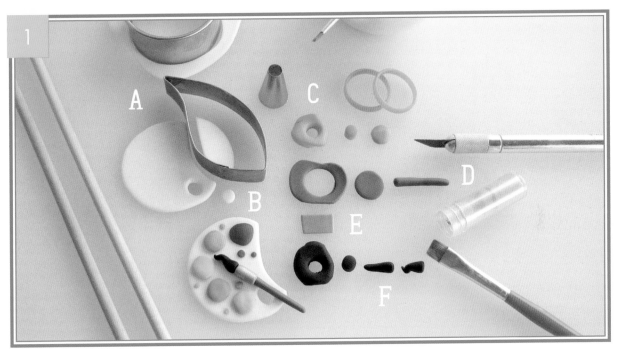

How to:

1. With the rolling pin, roll out white fondant ⅛ inch thick and cut out a 2¼-inch circle with the cutter. Use the inside arched side of the large leaf cutter to trim a piece off the circle to form the palette **(A)**. Round out the pointed edges. Use round tip #12 to cut a circle out of the tip of the palette **(B)**. For the paint, roll the different colors out thick with the rolling pin and wooden dowels and use round tip #12 to cut out one circle in each color. Roll them into balls and press them down a bit with your fingers to make uneven paint splotches **(C)**. Glue the paint to the paint palette. Pinch off very small pieces of each color, roll them into balls, and press them down a bit with your fingers. Glue the small pieces of paint next to the corresponding colors on the palette. With the rolling pin, roll out brown fondant ⅛ inch thick and use the bottom of round tip #12 to cut out a circle. Ball it up with your fingers and then roll it onto your work surface, narrowing one side a bit more to form the handle of the paintbrush **(D)**. With the rolling pin, roll out light gray fondant ⅛ inch thick. With the precision knife, cut out a small rectangle **(E)**. Brush it with silver shimmer dust and glue it over the wider end of the paintbrush handle. With the rolling pin and wooden dowels, roll out black fondant thick and use round tip #12 to cut out a circle. Ball it up and then shape it into a long cone. Coil the narrower end a bit to create the brush **(F)**. Glue it to the handle. Once the paintbrush is dry enough, glue it to the paint palette. Allow to dry thoroughly.

Art Supplies & Canvas

LEVEL OF DIFFICULTY

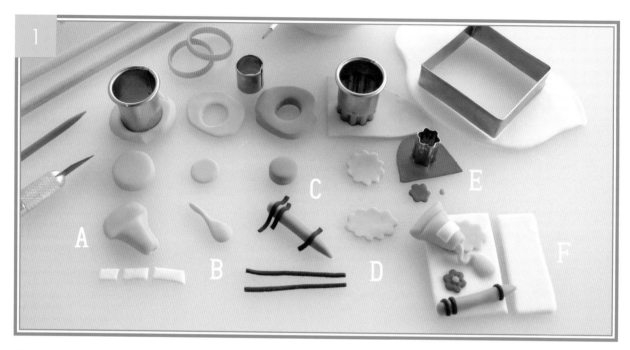

How to:

1. With the rolling pin and wooden dowels, roll out yellow fondant thick and cut out a circle with the ⅞-inch cutter. Ball up the circle and start shaping it into a tube, narrowing the top and flattening out the opposite wide end with your fingers. Roll up the wide, flattened end inward. Use the small modeling stick to make a hole at the narrow tip. With the rolling pin, roll out white fondant ¹⁄₁₆ inch thick and cut out a small rectangle with the precision knife for the label on the paint tube **(A)**. Glue the label to the tube. With the rolling pin, roll out yellow fondant ⅛ inch thick and cut out a small circle with the cutter. Roll it into a ball and then roll it out onto your work surface, leaving one end wider. Flatten the wide side a bit with your finger **(B)** and curl the remaining strip. Fit and glue the thin strip into the opening of the paint tube. With the rolling pin and wooden dowels, roll out green fondant thick and cut out a small circle with the cutter. Roll it out onto your work surface and narrow one end to shape a crayon. With the rolling pin, roll out black fondant ¹⁄₁₆ inch thick and cut out 3 narrow strips with the large square cutter. Form them over the crayon **(C)**, glue them, and trim the excess with the precision knife. With the rolling pin, roll out blue fondant ⅛ inch thick and cut out a circle with the ⅞-inch round scalloped circle. Lightly pull it apart with your fingers to make a cloud shape **(D)**. With the rolling pin, roll out red fondant ⅛ inch thick and cut out a flower with the small cutter **(E)**. Roll a very small circle with the orange fondant and glue it to the center of the red flower. Use the small modeling stick to make little indentations around the flower center. With the rolling pin, roll out white fondant ⅛ inch thick and cut out a large square with the cutter **(F)**. Trim it to a rectangular shape with the same cutter to form the canvas and glue all pieces on top. Allow to dry thoroughly.

SURF'S UP!

Materials Needed

fondant
(white, teal, yellow, sand & burnt orange)

black edible-ink marker

white soft gel paste

toothpick

1 orange stamen

Cutters Needed

7/8-inch circle cutter

round tips
#1, #7, #10 & #12

small circle cutter

large oval cutter

small & medium daisy cutters

small star cutter

Tools Needed

rolling pin with 1/8-inch & 1/16-inch guide rings

2 wooden dowels

knife tool

precision knife

modeling tool

small & large modeling sticks

small & medium ball tools

food scissors

rolling pastry cutter

Sweet Tips

SIMPLIFY
Decrease the number of fondant pieces, such as the crab, curly coral, and/or sand bucket/shovel.

ACCENTUATE
Accentuate your beach cupcakes with paper drink umbrellas. Be creative and make additional shells and sea life.

PERSONALIZE
Make initials and ages by cutting out fondant with the respective letter or number cutters and add a fish scale pattern.

EXPAND
Follow the striped topper tutorial in the Step Right Up collection (p. 72) but trim it into a rectangle for a beach towel.

DECORATE & DISPLAY
Embellish your cupcakes with blue frosting for water and add crushed graham crackers to represent sand. Use straw mats or cutting boards to display your cupcakes.

Beach Play

How to:

1. With the rolling pin, roll out white fondant ⅛ inch thick and cut out a large oval with the cutter. Spread a little bit of shortening over it and begin to stretch it from the top and bottom to form the surfboard. (Make sure you pull it slowly and evenly to avoid tearing or thinning in one area only. If you have a surfboard cutter, go ahead and use it!) Narrow the top a bit with your fingers and flatten the bottom **(A)**. With the rolling pin, roll out teal and yellow fondant 1/16 inch thick and use the rolling pastry cutter to cut strips, making sure the teal is wider than the yellow. Glue the strips to the surfboard **(B)**. Trim the excess as needed.

2. With the rolling pin and wooden dowels, roll out the teal fondant thick and cut out a ⅞-inch circle with the cutter. Roll it into a ball and then into a cylinder, narrowing the bottom. Use the medium ball tool to hollow out the center a little and re-form the bucket as needed **(A)**. With the rolling pin, roll out the sand fondant ⅛ inch thick and cut out a circle with the small cutter **(B)**. Round the sides out and fit it over the bucket. With the rolling pin, roll out teal and white fondant ⅛ inch thick and cut out a strip of each color with the rolling pastry cutter. Fit the teal strip around the top edge of the bucket, trim excess, and glue it. Glue the sand over the bucket. Trim the white strip and glue it to the bucket as the handle **(C)**. With the rolling pin, roll out yellow fondant ⅛ inch thick and cut out a circle with the ⅞-inch cutter. Roll it into a ball and then begin to roll it out onto your work surface, leaving one side wide for the shovel. Use the modeling tool to indent and widen the shovel. Punch a circle with round tip #1 out of the tip of the shovel handle **(D)**.

(continued on next page)

3. With the rolling pin and wooden dowels, roll out sand fondant thick and cut out a circle with the ⅞-inch cutter. Roll it into a ball and then into a cylinder and indent a window with the knife tool **(A)**. With the rolling pin, roll out more sand fondant ⅛ inch thick. Cut out 2 circles with the ⅞-inch cutter and 2 circles with the small circle cutter. Roll both larger circles into balls and shape them into cylinders. Indent one of them with the knife tool to make the window. Indent a couple of different windows in the second around the top. Use the small ball tool to indent the center of the latter **(B)**. Roll the 2 smaller circles into balls and then shape them into cones **(C)** and glue them to the tops of the flat castle towers. Glue the towers together. To make the crab, roll out burnt orange fondant thick with the rolling pin and wooden dowels and cut out a small circle with the cutter. Round out the sides with your finger and shortening and shape it into an oval **(D)**. Use round tip #10 to indent a smile on the side of the crab's face. With the thick burnt orange fondant, cut out 2 circles with round tip #10 and 6 circles with round tip #7. Shape the two larger circles into teardrops. Use the precision knife to cut along the center at the wider ends to make the crab claws **(E)**. Roll the remaining small circles onto your work surface and then pinch the ends and round them out to make the remaining crab legs **(F)**. With the food scissors, cut the orange stamen to fit into the crab's head. Draw eyes with the black edible-ink marker onto the stamens and use the white soft gel and a toothpick to dot the top of the eyes. Insert them into the crab **(G)**. Glue all the claws and legs to the crab. Allow to dry thoroughly.

Into the Sea

How to:

1. Roll out burnt orange fondant thick with the rolling pin and wooden dowels. Cut out a medium and small daisy with the cutters. With the medium-sized daisy, cut off 2 petals with the precision knife. With shortening on your fingers, begin to narrow and shape the coral (**A**). Do the same with the smaller daisy, but you do not need to remove any petals. Instead, push them to the side to flatten the bottom. With the rolling pin, roll out more burnt orange fondant ⅛ inch thick and cut out 2 more daisies, one of each size. Remove 1 petal from the larger daisy (**B**) and repeat the previous process for the smaller daisy. Allow them to dry overnight so they maintain their shape, and then glue the shapes together and stand them upright.

2. With the rolling pin and wooden dowels, roll out yellow fondant thick. Cut out 3 circles with the small cutter and shape them into cones, flattening the tip. Use the large modeling stick to hollow out the center of each coral. Make them different sizes and arrange and glue them together (**A**). With the rolling pin and wooden dowels, roll out sand fondant thick and cut out a star with the small cutter. Round out the sides of the star, indent the creases of the star, and pinch the tips with your fingers. Use the small modeling stick to make linear indentations from the center to the tips of the starfish arms (**B**). With the rolling pin, roll out burnt orange fondant ⅛ inch thick and cut out a small circle. Roll it into a ball. Then roll it out onto your work surface and spiral it into itself (**C**).

3. With the rolling pin and wooden dowels, roll out teal fondant thick and cut out a small circle with the cutter. Shape it into an oval, narrowing 1 side. Round it out and flatten it a bit with your fingers dipped in shortening. Use the precision knife to cut a slit at the narrow end to form the fish tail. Use tip #7 at a 45-degree angle to make indentations for a fish scale pattern (**A**). Indent a mouth for the fish. With the rolling pin, roll out teal fondant ⅛ inch thick and cut out a circle with round tip #12. Shape it into a teardrop and then coil the tip a bit. Use the knife tool to indent the wider end and glue the fin to the fish (**B**). Roll a very small piece of white fondant into a ball and flatten it for the fish eye. Use the black edible-ink marker to dot the eye and glue it to the fish. Allow to dry thoroughly.

NOW SHOWING

Materials Needed

fondant
(black, white, light gray, red & yellow)

silver & gold
shimmer dust
& brushes

yellow gel paste
& water

black edible-ink marker

2 lollipop sticks

Cutters Needed

$\frac{7}{8}$-inch circle cutter

round tips
#3, #10 & #12

small & large
star cutters

Tools Needed

rolling pin with
$\frac{1}{8}$-inch guide rings

2 wooden dowels

precision knife

small ball tool

small modeling stick

small spatula

foam block

rolling pastry cutter

Sweet Tips

SIMPLIFY
Remove the camera from the red carpet topper and the popcorn from the film topper.

ACCENTUATE
Cut out different-sized stars to decorate additional cupcakes. Make additional toppers to resemble tickets and use the black edible-ink marker to write "Admit One" on them.

PERSONALIZE
Instead of "Now Showing," change the wording to a name and/or age.

EXPAND
Follow the tutorial for the top hat from the Dapper Dad collection (p. 185) to create a black hat for a classic movie theme.

DECORATE & DISPLAY
Use popcorn boxes, movies, and film reels to accentuate your presentation. Add movie candy and chocolates to your display.

Film & Popcorn

LEVEL OF DIFFICULTY

How to:

1. With the rolling pin, roll out light gray fondant ⅛ inch thick and cut out 2 circles with the ⅞-inch cutter (**A**). On 1 of the circles, cut out 4 smaller circles with round tip #10 and indent the center with round tip #3 (**B**). Roll out black fondant a bit thicker and use the wider bottom of a round tip to cut out a circle (**C**). Brush silver shimmer dust on the light gray circles and, once dry enough, glue them together with the black circle sandwiched in the middle to create a film reel. With the rolling pin, roll out black and white fondant ⅛ inch thick and use the rolling pastry cutter to cut strips, ensuring the black is wider than the white. Form the black strip into a wave shape. Use the precision knife to cut small squares out of the white strip and glue them onto the black to create the film (**D**).

2. With the rolling pin and wooden dowels, roll out white fondant thick and use the ⅞-inch cutter to cut out a circle (**A**). Dip your fingers in shortening and mold the fondant to the shape of a popcorn box with a wider top and narrower bottom (**B**). With the rolling pin, roll out red fondant ⅛ inch thick and use the rolling pastry cutter to cut out 3 strips (**C**). Trim them to size over the popcorn box and glue them on. Cut off a piece of the bottom of the popcorn box so it will sit upright. Use the ball tool, foam block, and yellow gel paste and follow the tutorial to make popcorn from the Glam Sleepover collection (p. 38). Glue the popcorn to the top of the box (**D**). With the rolling pin, roll out red fondant ⅛ inch thick and cut out a large star with the cutter (**E**). Glue all the pieces together. Allow to dry thoroughly.

Marquee & Red Carpet

LEVEL OF DIFFICULTY

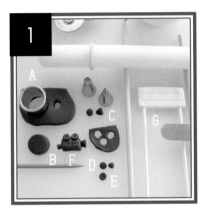

How to:

1. With the rolling pin and wooden dowels, roll out black fondant thick and cut 2 circles: 1 with the ⅞-inch cutter and the other with round tip #12 (**A**). With the larger circle, dip your fingers in shortening and form it into a rectangle to make a film camera (**B**). Form the smaller circle into a cone and then flatten both sides a bit (**C**). Glue it to the front of the camera. With the rolling pin, roll out black fondant ⅛ inch thick and cut out 3 circles with round tip #12. Roll 1 of them into a ball and then into a cone (**D**) and glue it to the back of the camera. Use round tip #3 to indent the center of the other 2 circles (**E**) and glue them toward the top of the camera. Use round tip #3 and the small modeling stick to make button indentations on the side of the camera (**F**). With the rolling pin and wooden dowels, roll out white fondant thick and cut out a rectangle (approximately 2 × 1½ inches). Insert 2 lollipop sticks on each side by carefully twisting upward, readjusting the fondant if necessary. Use the small spatula to make linear indentations on the front of the marquee (**G**).

2. With the rolling pin, roll out white and red fondant ⅛ inch thick. Cut a strip out of the red fondant with the rolling pastry cutter (approximately 1½ inches wide) and glue it over the white fondant. Cut out a large star with the cutter, with the red carpet down the center (**A**). With the rolling pin, roll out yellow and light gray fondant ⅛ inch thick and cut out about 7 small stars of each color with the small cutter. Brush the corresponding shimmer dusts onto the stars (**B**). Glue 2 stars, along with the camera, to the red carpet star (**C**). Use the black edible-ink marker to write "Now Showing" on the marquee and glue the remaining stars to it (**D**). Allow to dry thoroughly.

ROCK THE BEAT

Materials Needed

fondant
(white, red, black & light gray)

raw spaghetti

toothpick

Cutters Needed

⅞-inch & 2¼-inch
circle cutters

round tips #3, #7 & #12

medium & large
oval cutters

small circle cutter

large leaf cutter

small teardrop cutter

Tools Needed

rolling pin with
⅛-inch guide rings

2 wooden dowels

knife tool

precision knife

small modeling stick

dotted embossing mat

Sweet Tips

SIMPLIFY
Cut only the silhouette of the guitar and make indentations directly on it without added details. Omit the electrical cords from the headphones and microphone.

ACCENTUATE
Make records by rolling out black fondant and cutting a large circle. Use several circle cutters in descending size to make indentations on the record. Add a pop of color at the center. If you have a musical note cutter, cut them out in different colors and add to additional cupcakes.

PERSONALIZE
Add initials and/or ages to the center of the records (see above), or make CDs following the same steps as above with light gray fondant, but only make small circle indentations toward the center and cut a circle out of the middle. Use a black edible marker to write names on CDs.

EXPAND
Follow the tutorial for the word bubbles from the To the Rescue collection (p. 91) and replace the letters with "Rock."

DECORATE & DISPLAY
Embellish your presentation with records, musical instruments, and boom boxes.

Guitar

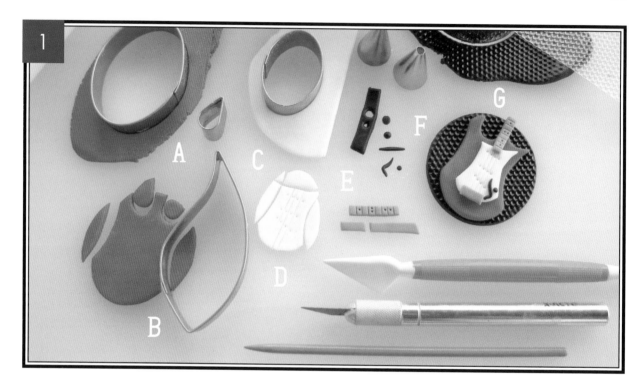

How to:

1. With the rolling pin, roll out red fondant ⅛ inch thick and cut out a large oval with the cutter (**A**). Use the large leaf cutter to trim the oval on both sides to start shaping the guitar. Use the wide end of the small teardrop cutter to trim the top, leaving a section for the guitar neck (**B**). With the rolling pin, roll out white fondant ⅛ inch thick and cut out a medium oval with the cutter (**C**). Use the large leaf cutter to trim the sides and top to form the pick guard, ensuring it fits properly over the guitar. Use the knife tool to indent the strings and pickups (**D**). Glue it to the guitar. With the rolling pin, roll out light gray fondant ⅛ inch thick. Cut out 2 strips with the precision knife. With the knife tool and small modeling stick, make indentations of the neck on 1 strip and trim it (**E**). Then glue it to the top of the guitar. Trim the second strip to a small rectangle and glue it toward the bottom of the pick guard. With the rolling pin, roll out black fondant ⅛ inch thick and cut out a circle with round tip #3 and another circle with round tip #7. Roll the larger circle into a ball and then roll it out onto your work surface. Fold up one end and coil the other end to form the whammy bar (**F**). Glue the whammy bar and smaller circle to the guitar. With the rolling pin, roll out more black fondant ⅛ inch thick and spread a bit of shortening over the fondant. Place the embossing mat over the fondant and use the rolling pin to impress the pattern onto it. Use the 2¼-inch cutter to punch out a circle and glue the guitar to it. Allow to dry thoroughly (**G**).

Headphones & Microphone

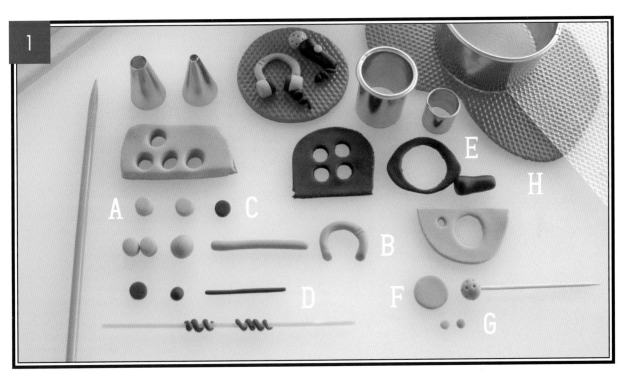

How to:

1. To make the headphones, roll out light gray fondant thick with the rolling pin and wooden dowels. Cut out 4 circles with round tip #12. Round out 2 of the circles and turn them on their sides for the earphones **(A)**. Use the small modeling stick to make a hole in one of the earphones to later insert the cord. Roll the other 2 circles together into a ball and then roll out onto your worktable. Shape the fondant into the headband and use the knife tool to make decorative indentations **(B)**. With the rolling pin, roll out black fondant ⅛ inch thick and cut out 4 circles with round tip #12 **(C)**. Use 2 of them as the inside ear cushions and glue them to the light gray earphones. Roll the other 2 into balls and then narrow them onto your worktable. Coil the cords around the raw spaghetti and allow them to dry sufficiently so they will hold their shapes **(D)**. When dry enough, insert and glue one end of one of the cord coils into the hole on the earphone and glue all headphone parts together. To make the microphone, roll out black fondant thick with the rolling pin and wooden dowels. Cut out a circle with the ⅞-inch cutter. Roll it into a ball and then shape it into the microphone

(continued on next page)

handle (a cone with flattened top and bottom) **(E)**. Use the small modeling stick to make a hole in the narrow end of the microphone handle to later insert the cord. Roll out light gray fondant with the rolling pin ⅛ inch thick and cut out a small circle with the cutter. Roll it into a ball and place it on the toothpick. While holding the toothpick, use the small modeling stick to make a pattern over the microphone speaker **(F)**. When complete, remove it from the toothpick and glue it to the microphone handle. Cut a small circle out of the light gray fondant with round tip #7. Roll it into a ball, and then flatten it a bit to make the microphone button **(G)**. Glue it to the microphone, along with the remaining coiled cord. With the rolling pin, roll out red fondant ⅛ inch thick and spread a bit of shortening over the fondant. Place the embossing mat over the fondant and use the rolling pin to impress the pattern onto it. Use the 2¼-inch cutter to punch out a circle **(H)** and glue the headphones and microphone to it. Allow to dry thoroughly.

NOTHING BUT NET

Materials Needed

fondant
*(orange, white, teal & black),
replace colors as needed
for desired team*

Cutters Needed

1¼-inch & 2¼-inch
circle cutters

Tools Needed

rolling pin with ⅛-inch
& 1/16-inch guide rings

2 wooden dowels

precision knife

small modeling stick

food scissors

rolling pastry cutter

dotted embossing mat

Sweet Tips

SIMPLIFY
Omit the basketball sneakers and replace with toppers with the team colors and names.

ACCENTUATE
Roll out fondant and cut out rectangular shapes for basketball courts. Indent rectangles, cut out fondant shapes, and/or use edible markers to make the lines on the court.

PERSONALIZE
Follow the tutorial for the Onesie in the Ooh La La collection (p. 225) but leave the bottom straight and trim off the sleeves to make jerseys. Add ages or initials to the front.

EXPAND
Follow the tutorial for the foam fingers in the Touchdown collection (p. 130) to accentuate additional cupcakes.

DECORATE & DISPLAY
Use wood plates and cutting boards that resemble basketball courts to display your cupcakes. Embellish your presentation with pom-poms and your team's paraphernalia.

Basketball Sneakers

LEVEL OF DIFFICULTY

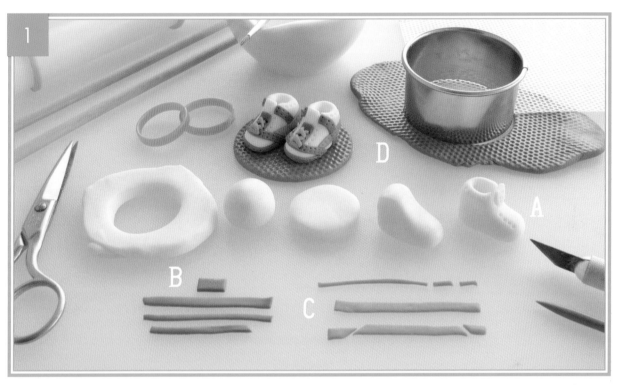

How to:

1. Roll out white fondant thick with the rolling pin and wooden dowels. Cut out a circle with the 1¼-inch cutter. Roll it into a ball and then shape it into an "L" with your fingers, making the bottom a bit longer. Dip your fingers in shortening and round out the sides a bit. Use the food scissors to cut 2 slits in the front for the shoe tongue. Use the small modeling stick to make stitching indentations (**A**). With the rolling pin, roll out teal fondant ¹⁄₁₆ inch thick and use the rolling pastry cutter to cut out different-sized strips for embellishing the sneakers (**B**). Fit them over the sneakers, trim them, and glue them. Use the small modeling stick to make indentations for stitches. With the rolling pin, roll out orange fondant ¹⁄₁₆ inch thick and use the rolling pastry cutter to cut a very thin strip. With the precision knife, cut out small strips for shoelaces. Layer them over the front of the sneakers, making "X" shapes, and glue them in place. Use the small modeling stick to create holes on each side of the shoelaces. Cut one last strip of orange fondant to embellish the side and back of the sneakers (**C**). With the rolling pin, roll out teal fondant ⅛ inch thick and spread a bit of shortening over the fondant. Place the dotted embossing mat over the fondant and use the rolling pin to impress the pattern onto it. Use the 2¼-inch cutter to punch out a circle and glue on the shoes (**D**). Allow to dry thoroughly.

Basketball

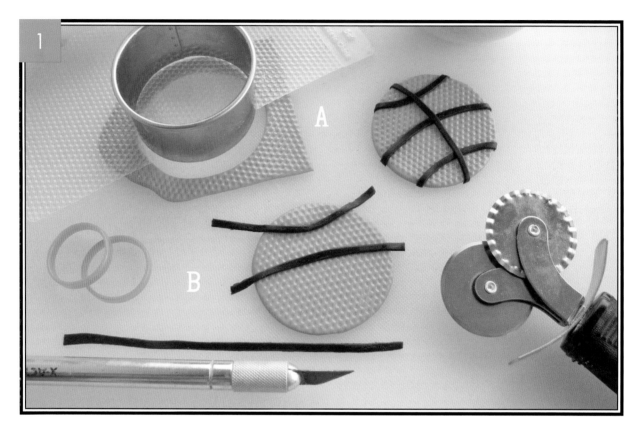

How to:

1. With the rolling pin, roll out orange fondant ⅛ inch thick and spread a bit of shortening over the fondant. Place the dotted embossing mat over the fondant and use the rolling pin to impress the pattern onto it **(A)**. Use the 2¼-inch cutter to punch out a circle and set it aside. With the rolling pin, roll out black fondant ¹⁄₁₆ inch thick and use the rolling pastry cutter to cut 4 strips. Fit them over the ball to form the basketball stripe markings, trim the excess with the precision knife, and glue them in place **(B)**. Allow to dry thoroughly.

TOUCHDOWN

fondant
*(brown, white & red),
replace colors as needed
for desired team*

lollipop stick

Cutters Needed

1½-inch circle cutter

round tips
#1 & #10

small & large
oval cutter

large hand cutter

Tools Needed

rolling pin with
⅛-inch guide rings

2 wooden dowels

rolling pastry cutter

precision knife

large ball tool

Sweet Tips

SIMPLIFY

Omit the football helmet from the collection.

ACCENTUATE

Cut out green fondant for grass and white strips for sidelines.
(You can personalize by adding an age for the sideline numbers.)

PERSONALIZE

Make triangular banners in the team's colors and add an initial.

EXPAND

Follow the tutorial to make a flag on a toothpick from the Fore collection (p. 138) without the argyle pattern to add to your assortment.

DECORATE & DISPLAY

Use green frosting and tip #233 to pipe grass onto your cupcakes. Look for cupcake liners and wrappers with football motifs. Use chalkboards with football plays drawn onto them with chalk to add to your presentation.

Football

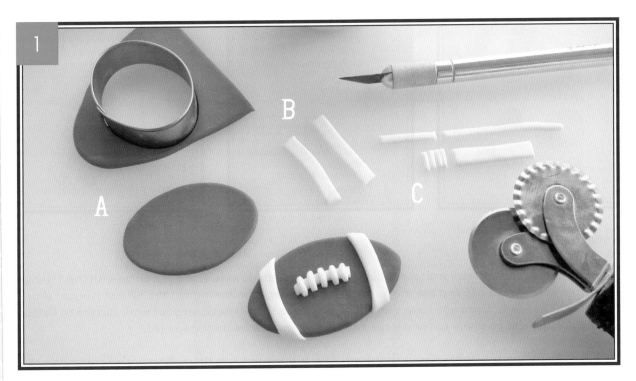

How to:

1. With the rolling pin, roll out brown fondant ⅛ inch thick and cut out an oval with the large cutter **(A)**. Gently pull the two ends apart to lengthen it and shape the ends to points to create the football. With the rolling pin, roll out white fondant ⅛ inch thick and use the rolling pastry cutter to cut 2 thick strips for the sides of the football **(B)**. Trim and glue them in place. Use the rolling pastry cutter to cut out thin strips. Glue 1 strip down the center of the football. Use the precision knife to cut out small strips **(C)**. Glue these little stitches over the middle strip. Allow to dry thoroughly.

Baseball

How to:

1. With the rolling pin, roll out white fondant ⅛ inch thick and cut out a 2¼-inch circle with the cutter **(A)**. Use the cutter to make 2 indentations on each side of the baseball to serve as guidelines for the stitches. With the rolling pin, roll out red fondant ⅛ inch thick and use the rolling pastry cutter to cut out a strip (approximately ½ inch wide). With the strip lying vertically over your work surface, use the corner of the large square cutter to trim about 10 "V" shapes to serve as stitches for the baseball **(B)**. Glue the stitches to the baseball, making sure the stitches go in the opposite direction of the other side. Use the 2¼-inch circle cutter to indent the center of the stitches **(C)**. Make sure not to apply too much glue/water so it does not seep through when indenting. Allow to dry thoroughly.

Baseball Field, Mitt & Bat

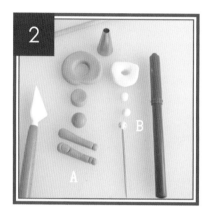

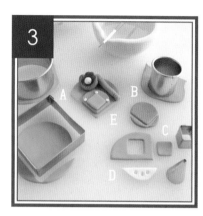

How to:

1. Roll out brown fondant thick with the rolling pin and wooden dowels. Cut out a small hand. Place the hand over the foam block and use the large ball tool to indent the center and shape it into the mitt. Use the knife tool to make indentations for the stitches around the baseball mitt. (If you do not have a hand cutter, cut out a circle and use the knife tool to indent the fingers.)

2. Roll out light brown fondant thick with the rolling pin and wooden dowels. Cut a circle with the bottom of round tip #10. Roll it into a ball and roll it onto your work surface, narrowing one end. Use the knife tool to make two indentations all the way around the bat, creating the base. Use round tip #10 to indent a circle at the top of the bat and the knife tool to make slight wood indentations **(A)**. Roll out white fondant thick with the rolling pin and wooden dowels. Cut out a circle with round tip #10. Roll it into a ball and then place it on a toothpick. Let it dry until it is hard enough to hold its shape and you can write on it. Use the red edible-ink marker to draw little "V" shapes for the baseball stitches, going in opposite directions **(B)**. When sufficiently dry, glue the baseball to the mitt.

3. With the rolling pin, roll out green fondant ⅛ inch thick and cut out a 2¼-inch circle with the cutter. Use the large square cutter to trim off a section of the fondant circle to make the baseball field **(A)**. With the rolling pin, roll out sand fondant ⅛ inch thick and cut out a 1¼-inch circle with the cutter. Use the large square cutter to trim off a section of the round fondant **(B)**. With the rolling pin, roll out additional green fondant ⅛ inch thick and cut out a small square with the cutter for the infield **(C)**. With the rolling pin, roll out white fondant ⅛ inch thick and use round tip #6 to cut out 3 circles for the bases **(D)**. Glue all pieces of the baseball field together and add the baseball mitt and bat **(E)**. Allow to dry thoroughly.

FORE!

fondant
*(white, blue, light blue,
green, black & light gray)*

silver shimmer
dust & brush

toothpicks

Cutters Needed

2¼-inch circle cutter

round tips
#3, #7 & #10

small circle cutter

small diamond cutter

medium oval cutter

large leaf cutter

medium hand cutter

Tools Needed

rolling pin with ⅛-inch
& 1/16-inch guide rings

precision knife

small modeling stick

small spatula

rolling pastry cutter

fondant storage board

Sweet Tips

SIMPLIFY	Avoid making the argyle pattern and use simple colors.
ACCENTUATE	With the hand cutter, punch additional hands out of white fondant for additional gloves. Roll semicircles and indent them with a small ball tool to create golf balls or indent flat, white toppers.
PERSONALIZE	Add ages or initials to the flags or create them with the golf ball path.
EXPAND	Modify the canvas and crayon tutorial from the Work of Art collection (p. 108) to create a pad of paper and a small pencil.
DECORATE & DISPLAY	Use green frosting and decorating tip #233 to pipe grass onto your cupcakes. Embellish your display with golf balls, faux grass, and tees.

Argyle Golf

How to:

1. With the rolling pin, roll out white, blue, light blue, and green fondant (one at a time) ⅛ inch thick and cut out small diamonds with the small cutter. Place them under the fondant storage board to avoid drying out (**A**). Once all colors have been cut out, with the rolling pin roll out white fondant ¹⁄₁₆ inch thick. Glue on the diamonds in an argyle pattern, and then turn the small spatula on its side and indent diagonal lines in the center of the diamonds (**B**). Repeat in the opposite direction and cut out a 2¼-inch circle with the cutter (**C**). Save extra of the argyle pattern to utilize for the golf glove and the flag—jump ahead to cut out the argyle shapes or save them in the fondant storage board (or clear ziplock bag) until you are ready to use them.

2. With the rolling pin, roll out white fondant ⅛ inch thick and cut out a hand with the medium cutter (**A**). Using the small circle cutter, cut out a slice of the hand. Use the medium oval cutter to indent the glove and the small modeling stick to make little dot indentations on the glove fingers (**B**). Cut a small circle with the cutter out of the extra argyle pattern and use the hand cutter to cut out a piece to fit into the side of the glove (**C**). With the rolling pin, roll out light gray fondant ⅛ inch thick. With round tip #7, cut out a circle and use round tip #3 to indent the middle of that circle (**D**). In the light gray fondant, cut out 2 circles with the small circle cutter. For the club, roll 1 circle into a ball, shape it into a teardrop, and use the precision knife to indent grooves. Use the small modeling stick to make a hole in the club (**E**) to insert the handle. Roll the second circle into a ball and roll it onto your work surface to create the handle (**F**). Use the silver shimmer dust to brush the club, handle, and glove button (**G**). Switch out the guide rings on the rolling pin and roll out black fondant ¹⁄₁₆ inch thick. Cut out a strip with the rolling pastry cutter and lay it over the end of the handle. Use the precision knife to trim it to size and glue it to form a grip, tucking the sides underneath. Make little indentations on the grip (**H**). Roll a small piece of white fondant into a ball and stick it onto a toothpick. Use the small modeling stick to indent little holes around it to create the golf ball. When complete, remove it from the toothpick and adjust the shape, if necessary (**I**). Glue all pieces together and onto the argyle topper. Allow to dry thoroughly.

Golf Green

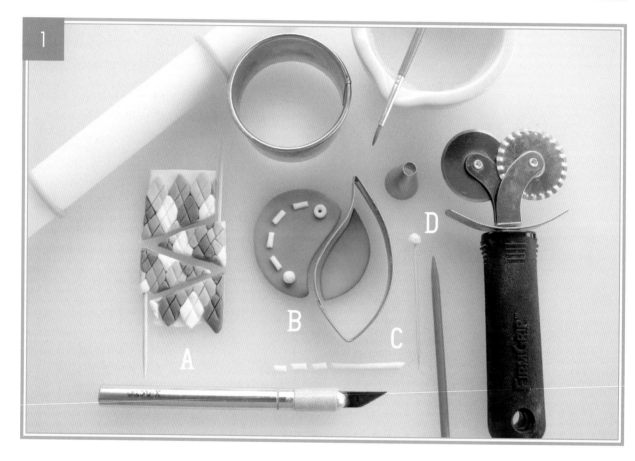

How to:

1. Use the saved argyle pattern (or see the argyle golf tutorial, p. 137) to cut out pennant flags with the rolling pastry cutter. Insert a toothpick by slowly rotating it into the wide side of the flag and allow to dry (**A**). With the rolling pin, roll out green fondant ⅛ inch thick and cut out a 2¼-inch circle with the cutter. Use the leaf cutter to cut out a portion of the green fondant, creating the golf green, and round out the ends with your finger dipped in shortening (**B**). With the rolling pin, roll out white fondant ⅛ inch thick and cut out a circle with round tip #10 for the golf hole where the flag will be inserted. Use the rolling pastry cutter to cut a thin strip out of the white fondant. Use the precision knife to cut out small lines to create the golf ball's path (**C**). Roll a small piece of white fondant into a ball and stick it onto a toothpick. Use the small modeling stick to indent little holes around it to create the golf ball (**D**). When complete, remove it from the toothpick and adjust the shape, if necessary. Glue all the pieces to the green topper and insert the flag into the hole. Allow to dry thoroughly.

JUST FOR KICKS

Materials Needed

fondant
*(black, white, red, yellow,
light gray & green)*

silver shimmer
dust & brush

2 lollipop sticks

Cutters Needed

small square cutter

1⅞-inch circle cutter

"G" letter cutter

Tools Needed

rolling pin with ⅛-inch
& 1/16-inch guide rings

2 wooden dowels

knife tool

precision knife

small modeling stick

rolling pastry cutter

fondant storage board

Sweet Tips

SIMPLIFY	Instead of cutting out the shapes on the soccer ball, draw them on with a black edible-ink marker.
ACCENTUATE	Cut out larger red and yellow cards to decorate additional cupcakes. Make soccer fields out of green fondant and make white lines with fondant or royal icing.
PERSONALIZE	Make flags and use appropriate team colors and initials and ages.
EXPAND	Follow the pants tutorial from the Beary Sweet Baby collection (p. 221) to make soccer shorts by making them shorter and not adding the rear design.
DECORATE & DISPLAY	Pipe the cupcakes with green frosting using tip #233 to make grass.

Soccer Ball

$\mathcal{How\ to:}$

1. Roll out white fondant ⅛ inch thick and cut out about 10 small squares with the cutter. Use the precision knife to cut the squares into hexagons (trimming 4 sides) **(A)** and place them inside the fondant storage board to save for later. Roll out black fondant ⅛ inch thick and cut out 6 small squares with the cutter. Use the precision knife to cut the squares into pentagons (trimming 4 sides) **(B)** and place them inside the fondant storage board as well. With the rolling pin, roll out white fondant 1/16 inch thick. Spread glue over the fondant and glue a black pentagon in the center. Then glue 5 white hexagons around the perimeter of the center pentagon. You might have to dip your finger in shortening and spread/shape the white hexagons so that they fit perfectly. Then glue the remaining white and black shapes around the perimeter, spreading them out more with your fingers dipped in shortening to make them fit. Use the 1⅞-inch circle cutter to trim the soccer ball. Use the small modeling stick to make indentations on the perimeter of the white hexagons **(C)**. Allow to dry thoroughly.

Referee

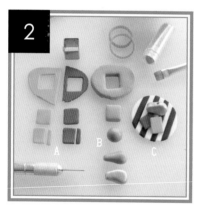

How to:

1. With the rolling pin, roll out white and black fondant ⅛ inch thick and use the rolling pastry cutter to cut out linear strips. Store them in the fondant storage board (**A**). With the rolling pin, roll out white fondant 1/16 inch thick and spread glue over it. Adhere the black and white strips, alternating the colors. Once complete, cut a 1⅞-inch circle with the cutter out of the striped pattern (**B**).

2. With the rolling pin, roll out yellow and red fondant ⅛ inch thick and cut out a small square of each color with the cutter. Use the precision knife to trim them into rectangles for the yellow and red cards (**A**). With the rolling pin and wooden dowels, roll out light gray fondant thick and cut out a small square with the cutter. Roll it into a ball and narrow one end. Square the narrow end off a bit and shape it into a whistle. Use the knife tool to indent the front and top of the whistle and brush it with silver shimmer dust (**B**). Glue the cards and whistle to the striped bottom topper (**C**). Allow to dry thoroughly.

Goal Sign

LEVEL OF DIFFICULTY

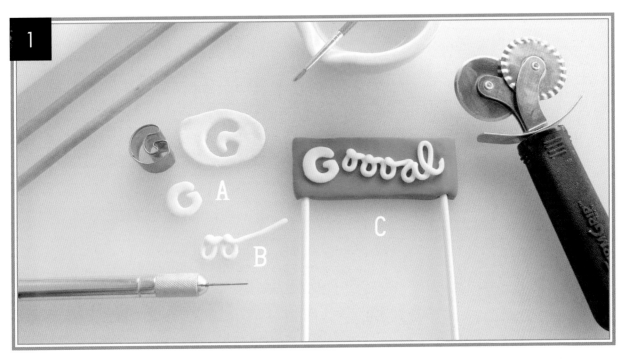

How to:

1. With the rolling pin, roll out white fondant ⅛ inch thick and cut out a G with the letter cutter **(A)**. Roll out additional white fondant onto your work surface until it is long and thin. Start shaping it into a few cursive Os **(B)** and then end it with an A and L. Roll out green fondant thick with the rolling pin and wooden dowels. With the rolling pastry cutter, trim the green fondant into a rectangle long enough to fit the letters. Insert the 2 lollipop sticks into each end by slowly twisting them in while re-forming the fondant with your fingers as needed. Glue the word to the sign **(C)**. Allow to dry thoroughly.

START YOUR ENGINES

Materials Needed

fondant
(red, green, white, black & yellow)

lollipop sticks

Cutters Needed

⅞-inch & 2¼-inch circle cutters

round tips
#2, #6, #10 & #12

small leaf cutter

small square cutter

Tools Needed

rolling pin with ⅛-inch & ¹⁄₁₆-inch guide rings

2 wooden dowels

precision knife

modeling stick

rolling pastry cutter

fondant storage board

Sweet Tips

SIMPLIFY
Omit the three-dimensional car and spread out the stoplight and spare tires.

ACCENTUATE
Cover additional cupcakes with dark gray fondant and add track lines. Roll out black fondant thick with the rolling pin and wooden dowels and cut a long rectangle. Insert two lollipop sticks on each end to make a sign. Cut out the word "Finish" with white fondant and letter cutters and glue together.

PERSONALIZE
Punch initials and/or ages out of dark gray fondant with respective cutters and add small white lines to resemble a street/track.

EXPAND
Follow the tutorial to make construction cones from the Under Construction collection (p. 94) in yellow to add to your assortment.

DECORATE & DISPLAY
Enhance your cupcakes with checkerboard liners and party supplies.

Stoplight & Spare Tires

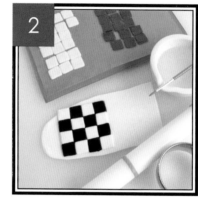

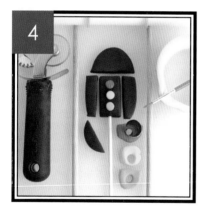

How to:

1. With the rolling pin, roll out black and white fondant ⅛ inch thick and cut out small squares with the cutter. Place them inside the fondant storage board to avoid drying out.

2. With the rolling pin, roll out white fondant 1/16 inch thick. Spread glue onto the thin fondant and start placing the square black and white pieces to create a checkerboard pattern. Utilize the 2¼-inch circle cutter to punch out the bottom of the topper. Insert a lollipop stick to make a hole before it dries to later insert the stoplight.

3. Using the wooden dowels and the rolling pin, roll out black fondant thick and cut out 3 circles with the ⅞-inch cutter (A). With your fingers, round out the sides of the tires and cut a hole out of the center with round tip #10. Utilize the diagonal edge of the small square cutter to make tread indentations around the entire tire (B).

4. With the rolling pin and wooden dowels, roll out a large piece of black fondant thick, as well as small pieces of red, yellow, and green fondant. With the rolling pastry cutter, cut out a rectangle for the stoplight and insert a lollipop stick through the bottom, reshaping as needed. With round tip #10, cut a circle out of each of the colors and glue onto the stoplight to make the lights. Glue the tires to the checkerboard topper. Once completely dry, insert the stoplight into the hole.

Race Car

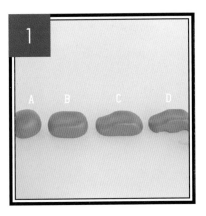

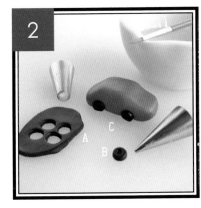

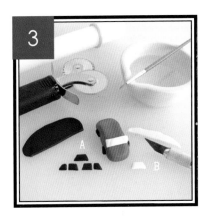

How to:

1. Roll some red fondant into a ball (approximately 1 inch) (**A**). With your fingers dabbed in shortening, mold the ball into a rectangle (**B**) and proceed to smooth your fingers over the back to make a small diagonal slant. On the front of the car, flatten out an area for the hood as well as another diagonal slant for the windshield (**C**). With round tip #12, make 4 marks (2 on each side) and utilize the modeling stick to indent the inside of the circles to fit the tires (**D**).

2. With a rolling pin, roll out black fondant ⅛ inch thick. With round tip #12, cut out 4 circles (**A**). Indent the middle of the tires with round tip #2 (**B**). Glue the tires into the sections of the car, turning the front ones slightly (**C**).

3. With a rolling pin, roll out black fondant ⅛ inch thick and use the rolling pastry cutter to cut a ¼-inch-wide line. With the precision knife, cut out the back and side windows (**A**). Do the same with white fondant for the front windshield (**B**). You can place it on the car to measure and score the fondant prior to cutting. Glue the windshield and windows onto the car.

(continued on next page)

(continued):

4. With the rolling pin, roll out white fondant ⅛ inch thick and utilize round tips #2 and #6 to cut out accent pieces for the car **(A)**. Cut out rectangles and indent them to make bumpers and grilles. Roll out yellow fondant on the table with your fingers and mold it into a desired number **(B)**. With a rolling pin, roll more yellow fondant ⅛ inch thick and use the small leaf cutter to punch out 2 shapes. Use the precision knife to cut off the rounded end and pointed side of the leaf cutter to cut small sections, shaping it into a flame **(C)**. Glue all pieces to the car and allow to dry thoroughly. Repeat the steps from the stoplight and spare tires tutorial (p. 146) to make the checkerboard topper and glue the car onto it when complete.

SNOWBALL PENGUIN

Materials Needed

fondant
*(black, white, pink,
light blue & orange)*

white soft gel paste

toothpick

raw spaghetti

Cutters Needed

⅞-inch, 1¼-inch &
1½-inch circle cutters

round tips
#5, #10 & #12

small, medium &
large teardrop cutters

medium heart cutter

Tools Needed

rolling pin with ⅛-inch
& 1/16-inch guide rings

2 wooden dowels

knife tool

precision knife

rolling pastry cutter

food scissors

Sweet Tips

SIMPLIFY	Make a flat penguin face instead of a three-dimensional figure.
ACCENTUATE	Roll several additional snowballs out of white fondant to accentuate the cupcake and decorate additional ones. Use white shimmer dust to brush onto the penguin's snowball and the extras. Make penguins in different positions (sliding, on their bellies, with snowballs thrown on their heads/bodies, and so on) for additional cupcakes.
PERSONALIZE	Cut large circles out of white fondant to make flat snowballs, dust them with white shimmer, and glue cut-out ages or letters to them.
EXPAND	Add some of the elements from the Christmas toppers, such as the reindeer (p. 207), to the penguin assortment.
DECORATE & DISPLAY	Add white frosting to resemble snow. Add to your presentation with white gumballs, sugar cubes, and cotton candy.

Cozy Penguin

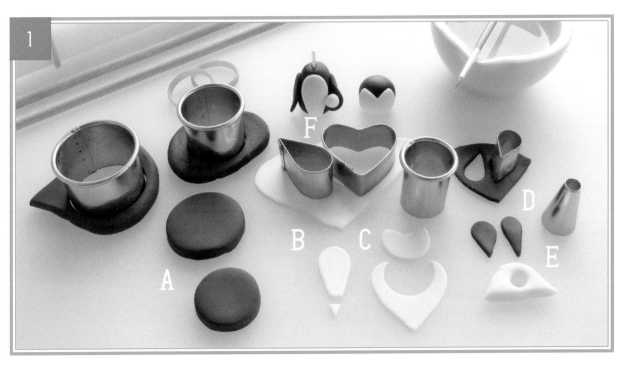

How to:

1. Roll out black fondant thick with the rolling pin and wooden dowels. Cut out a 1¼-inch circle and a 1½-inch circle with the respective cutters **(A)**. Roll the larger circle into a ball and then into an oval to shape the body. Insert a piece of raw spaghetti through the center by carefully twisting through, leaving enough protruding to hold the head. Roll the second circle into a ball to form the penguin's head and make a hole with the raw spaghetti to later be inserted over the body. With the rolling pin, roll white fondant ⅟₁₆ inch thick and cut out a large teardrop shape and medium heart with the cutters. Trim the pointed end off the teardrop shape **(B)** and glue it to the front of the penguin's body. Use the ⅞-inch cutter to cut out a circle at the top center of the heart **(C)** and glue it to the penguin's face. With the rolling pin, roll out black fondant ⅛ inch thick and cut out 2 medium teardrops. Stretch them out a bit by carefully pulling the ends apart for the wings **(D)**. Roll out white fondant thick with the rolling pin and wooden dowels. Cut out a small circle with round tip #12 **(E)**. Roll it into a snowball and wrap the tip of one of the wings around it. Glue the snowball to the wing, and then glue the wings to the side of the penguin **(F)**. When the body is firm enough, insert the penguin's head through the spaghetti and glue it in place.

(continued on next page)

(continued):

2. With the rolling pin, roll out orange fondant ⅛ inch thick. Cut out 2 small teardrop shapes with the cutter and 1 circle with round tip #10. Use the knife tool make 2 indentations on the wide end of the teardrop shapes for the penguin feet. With the round tip, trim off the pointed ends **(A)** and glue the feet to the penguin. Shape the small circle into a ball and then into a cone to make the penguin's beak **(B)** and glue it to the face. With the rolling pin, roll out black fondant ⅛ inch thick and cut out 2 circles with round tip #5 for the eyes **(C)**. Glue the eyes to the penguin's face, and then dip the toothpick in white soft gel paste and dot the eyes. With the rolling pin, roll out pink fondant ⅛ inch thick and use the rolling pastry cutter to cut a 4-inch strip. Cut 3 small lines at each end with the precision knife to make the scarf fringe and indent the remainder of the strip with the knife tool. Wrap the scarf around the penguin and glue it in place **(D)**. Roll out light blue fondant thick with the rolling pin and wooden dowels. Cut out a circle with round tip #10. Use the food scissors to make little cuts around the entire ball to make a little pom-pom and glue it to the scarf where both sides meet **(E)**. With the rolling pin, roll out light blue fondant ⅛ inch thick. Cut out a ⅞-inch circle with the cutter and form it over the penguin's head. Roll out pink fondant thick with the rolling pin and wooden dowels. Cut out a circle with round tip #12. Use the food scissors to make little cuts around the entire ball to make a pom-pom for the cap **(F)** and glue it in the center. With the rolling pin, roll out pink fondant ⅛ inch thick and cut out a narrow strip with the rolling pastry cutter. Make small indentations across the strip with the knife tool and shape it around the bottom of the cap. Trim it to size and glue it in place **(G)**. Glue the cap to the penguin's head. Allow to dry thoroughly.

BOOKWORM

Materials Needed

fondant
*(green, red, blue, orange,
yellow, black, brown
& light brown)*

Cutters Needed

1½-inch circle cutter

2¼-inch scalloped
circle cutter

round tips
#5, #7 & #12

small teardrop cutter

small circle cutter

Tools Needed

rolling pin with
⅛-inch guide rings

2 wooden dowels

knife tool

precision knife

small modeling stick

rolling pastry cutter

linear embossing mat

Sweet Tips

SIMPLIFY	Omit the glasses and the book from the bookworm.
ACCENTUATE	Make additional blackboards for additional cupcakes and cut out numbers or letters to add on top. Make bigger books to decorate additional cupcakes.
PERSONALIZE	With white fondant and the linear embossing mat, make additional toppers to resemble lined paper. Cut out an "A," and glue the grade to the paper to embellish additional cupcakes, or use initials or ages.
EXPAND	Add elements from the Work of Art collection (p. 105), such as paint, crayons, and palettes.
DECORATE & DISPLAY	Embellish your presentation with everyday school supplies, such as a blackboard as a cupcake display.

Bookworm

LEVEL OF DIFFICULTY

How to:

1. Roll red fondant thick with the rolling pin and wooden dowels. Cut a 1½-inch circle with the cutter. Roll it into a ball and then shape it into an apple by narrowing the bottom **(A)**. Use the small modeling stick to make a hole in the center. With the rolling pin, roll out green fondant ⅛ inch thick and cut out a leaf with the small teardrop cutter. Use the knife tool to indent the leaf veins **(B)**. With the rolling pin, roll out brown fondant ⅛ inch thick and cut out a small circle with round tip #12. Roll it into a ball and then roll it onto your work surface, narrowing the tip just a bit to form the stem **(C)**. Glue the leaf and stem into the top of the apple. With the rolling pin, roll out green fondant ⅛ inch thick and cut out a small circle with the cutter. Roll it into a ball **(D)**. Repeat the last step with yellow, blue, red, and orange fondant. Glue the balls together to form the bookworm. With the rolling pin, roll out black fondant ⅛ inch thick and cut out 2 circles with round tip #12 for the glasses and 2 with round tip #5 for the eyes. With the #12-sized circles, use round tip #7 to punch out the center to form the glasses **(E)** and glue them to the bookworm's face. Then glue the eyes to the center of the glasses.

2. With the rolling pin, roll out white fondant ⅛ inch thick and use the rolling pastry cutter to cut a strip (approximately ⅓ inch wide). Trim a rectangle with the precision knife and use the knife tool to indent the center to form the book pages **(A)**. With the rolling pin, roll out yellow fondant ⅛ inch thick and use the rolling pastry cutter to cut a strip a bit bigger than the white. Make 2 indentations towards the center to form the book binding and cover **(B)**. Turn the yellow cover over and glue in the white pages to form the book. With the rolling pin, roll out green fondant ⅛ inch thick and use round tip #7 to cut out 2 circles. Roll them into balls and then use the knife tool to

(continued on next page)

(continued):

indent the center to form the bookworm's hands **(C)**. Glue the hands to the side of the book with the indented center around the edge of the book cover and stand the book up **(D)**. With the rolling pin, roll out white fondant ⅛ inch thick and spread a bit of shortening over the fondant. Place the linear embossing mat over the fondant and use the rolling pin to impress the pattern onto it. Use the 2¼-inch scalloped cutter to punch out a circle **(E)**. Glue the apple, bookworm, and book to the topper, with the topper lines going horizontally to resemble a lined piece of paper. Allow to dry thoroughly.

School Supplies

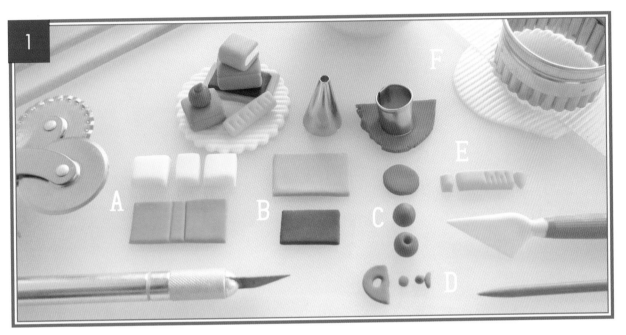

How to:

1. Roll out white fondant thick with the rolling pin and wooden dowels. Trim 3 rectangles in different sizes with the rolling pastry cutter to form the book pages. With the rolling pin, roll out green, orange, and blue fondant ⅛ inch thick and trim them with the rolling pastry cutter slightly larger than the respective white pages to form the book covers. Use the knife tool to make 2 indentations for the book bindings (A) on each book cover. Glue all the book covers to the pages. With the rolling pin, roll out light brown fondant ⅛ inch thick and use the rolling pastry cutter to cut a rectangle (approximately 1½ inches long by ¾ inch wide). With the rolling pin, roll out black fondant ⅛ inch thick and use the rolling pastry cutter to trim a rectangle smaller than the light brown to form the blackboard (B) and glue the pieces together. With the rolling pin, roll out red fondant ⅛ inch thick and cut out a small circle with the cutter. Roll it into a ball, narrow the bottom, and make a hole in the top with the small modeling stick (C). With the rolling pin, roll out brown fondant ⅛ inch thick and cut out a small circle with round tip #7. Roll it into a ball and then roll it onto your work surface to make the apple stem (D). Glue it into the top of the apple. Roll out yellow fondant thick with the rolling pin and wooden dowels. Use the rolling pastry cutter to trim a long rectangle to form the ruler. Use the knife tool to make measurement indentations (E). With the rolling pin, roll out white fondant ⅛ inch thick and spread a bit of shortening over the fondant. Place the linear embossing mat over the fondant and use the rolling pin to impress the pattern onto it. Use the 2¼-inch scalloped cutter to punch out a circle (F) and glue on the blackboard, books, apple, and ruler with the topper lines going horizontally to resemble a lined piece of paper. Allow to dry thoroughly.

CONGRATS, GRAD!

Materials Needed

fondant
*(black, white, school color #1
& school color #2)*

lollipop sticks

Styrofoam block

Cutters Needed

2¼-inch circle cutter

round tips
#1, #7 & #12

number cutters
(graduation year)

Tools Needed

rolling pin with
⅛-inch guide rings

2 wooden dowels

precision knife

rolling pastry cutter

Sweet Tips

SIMPLIFY
Omit the lollipop stick and make a graduation cap to glue directly to the fondant topper.

ACCENTUATE
Make the graduation caps on different-sized lollipop sticks in various positions to look like caps being thrown up in the air.

PERSONALIZE & EXPAND
Follow the book tutorial from the Bookworm collection (p. 157) and add initials to personalize them for additional cupcakes.

DECORATE & DISPLAY
Locate graduation-themed cupcake liners and confetti to enhance your display. Present your cupcakes on actual books and roll up papers to look like diplomas.

Graduation

How to:

1. Roll black fondant thick with the rolling pin and wooden dowels. Use the bottom of a round tip to punch out a circle and round it out (**A**). Insert the circle into the end of a lollipop stick at an angle. Insert the lollipop stick into the Styrofoam block to dry. With the rolling pin, roll out black fondant ⅛ inch thick and use the rolling pastry cutter to cut a square a little less than 1 inch (**B**). In the black fondant, punch out a small circle with round tip #7 and set it aside to later glue it to the center of the graduation cap (**C**). With the rolling pin, roll out school color #1 to ⅛ inch thick and cut out a circle with round tip #12. Roll it into a ball and then onto your work surface, leaving one end a bit wider. Use the precision knife to cut a few strips on the wide end to form the tassel (**D**). When the black square is dry enough, glue it to the graduation cap on the lollipop stick and then add the tassel and black circle on top of the center. Return it to the Styrofoam block to dry (**E**). With the rolling pin, roll out white fondant ⅛ inch thick and trim a rectangle with the rolling pastry cutter (approximately 1¼ inches long by 1 inch wide). Hold the corners of one end and gently pull them apart so they stick out a bit. Then start rolling that end into itself to form the diploma and round it out a little (**F**). With the rolling pin, roll out school color #1 to ⅛ inch thick and cut out a strip with the rolling pastry cutter. Glue it over the center of the diploma, trim the sides, and tuck it under. Cut out a circle with round tip #7 of the same colored fondant (**G**) and glue it to the center of the strip on the diploma to form the seal. Use round tip #1 to indent the center of the seal. With the rolling pin, roll out school color #2 to ⅛ inch thick and cut out the graduating year with the number cutters (**H**). With the rolling pin, roll out black fondant ⅛ inch thick and cut out a 2¼-inch circle with the cutter. Glue the year and diploma to the topper and insert a lollipop stick to make a hole (**I**) to later insert the graduation cap when decorating your cupcake. Allow to dry thoroughly.

WE GO TOGETHER LIKE PEAS & CARROTS

Materials Needed

fondant
(orange, green, black, pink & red)

Cutters Needed

1⅞-inch circle cutter

round tips
#2, #3 & #7

small teardrop cutter

large heart cutter

small heart cutter

Tools Needed

rolling pin with
⅛-inch guide rings

2 wooden dowels

knife tool

 Sweet Tips

SIMPLIFY	Omit the faces to make the shapes easier or draw them on with edible-ink markers.
ACCENTUATE	Create additional toppers with the heart shapes in pinks and reds for extra cupcake decor.
PERSONALIZE	Cut out initials of the couple and add them to simple fondant hearts.
EXPAND	Grow a love garden with the addition of lettuce from the Hoppy Easter collection (p. 173) (which can also resemble a flower).
DECORATE & DISPLAY	Present the cupcakes in individual cupcake boxes as gifts with matching ribbon or present them on heart-shaped plates with Valentine decor.

Peas & Carrots

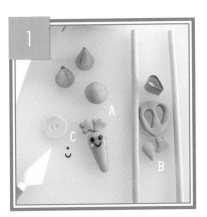

1

How to:

1. Roll orange fondant into a ball (approximately ¾ inch) and roll it out with your fingers, narrowing one end to form the carrot **(A)**. Roll out green fondant thick with the rolling pin and wooden dowels. Cut out 2 shapes with the small teardrop cutter. Use the knife tool to make 2 indentations on the larger sides to create the shoots **(B)** and glue to the top of the carrot. With the rolling pin, roll out black fondant ⅛ inch thick. Cut out 2 circles with round tip #7 for the eyes and one circle with round tip #3. Roll the latter circle into a ball and then roll it out onto your work surface. Curl both ends upward to form the mouth. With the rolling pin, roll out pink fondant ⅛ inch thick and cut out 2 circles with round tip #3 for the cheeks. Glue all pieces to the carrot's face **(C)**.

2

2. Roll 3 pieces of green fondant into balls (approximately ⅜ inch) to make the peas. With the rolling pin, roll out black fondant ⅛ inch thick and cut out 9 circles with round tip #3. Save 6 of the circles for the eyes. With the remaining 3, repeat the step from the carrot to create the pea mouths. With the rolling pin, roll out pink fondant ⅛ inch thick and cut out 6 circles with round tip #2 for the pea cheeks **(A)**. Glue all components to the 3 peas. With the rolling pin, roll out green fondant ⅛ inch thick and cut out a circle with the 1⅞-inch cutter. Fold it over, pinching the sides together but ensuring the opening remains wide enough to fit the peas **(B)**. Glue the peas to the bottom and fit the top of the peapod over their heads, ensuring their faces are peeking out enough. With the rolling pin, roll out pink and red fondant ⅛ inch thick. Cut a large heart out of the pink fondant with the cutter **(C)** and a smaller heart out of the red with the cutter. Use your fingers to pinch and curl the bottom of the small heart **(D)**. Glue all pieces together and allow to dry thoroughly.

LOVE BUGS

Materials Needed

fondant
(black, red & white)

2 white stamens

black & white soft gel paste & brush

raw spaghetti

toothpicks

Cutters Needed

1¼-inch circle cutter

round tips #7 & #10

large scalloped heart cutter

medium heart cutter

Tools Needed

rolling pin with ⅛-inch guide rings

2 wooden dowels

knife tool

food scissors

Sweet Tips

SIMPLIFY	Make smaller bugs with a small red body lying on the bottom topper and indent the eyes and mouths.
ACCENTUATE	Cut out additional large hearts and add larger black spots to the bugs.
PERSONALIZE	Add the couple's initials punched out of fondant with letter cutters and glue them to red and white hearts.
EXPAND	Follow the tutorial to make bees from the Queen Bee collection (p. 65) to add more bugs to the assortment.
DECORATE & DISPLAY	Use little tins or pots to display or gift the cupcakes. Or find polka-dot boxes, plates, or paper for your presentation.

Love Bugs

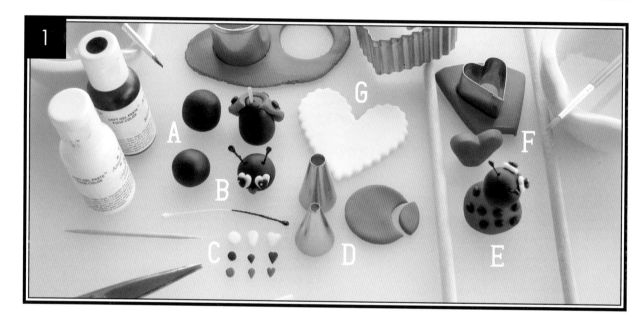

How to:

1. Roll black fondant into balls for the bug bodies (2 at approximately ¾ inch) and heads (2 at approximately ⅝ inch). Roll the bodies into oval shapes and sit them on the work surface. Insert raw spaghetti into the bodies, leaving enough protruding to hold up the heads **(A)**. Using black soft gel paste, paint the white stamens. When dry, cut them with the food scissors and insert them into the bugs' heads **(B)**. With the rolling pin, roll out white, black, and red fondant ⅛ inch thick. Use round tip #10 to cut 4 circles out of the white fondant. Use tip #7 to cut 4 circles out of the black fondant and 2 out of the red fondant. Shape them into teardrops and indent the tops with the knife tool to form hearts **(C)**. Glue the black hearts to the white, creating the eyes. Glue them, as well as the red mouths, to the bugs' faces. Use the toothpick dipped in the white soft gel paste to dab little spots on the eyes, making sure both bugs are looking at each other. With the rolling pin, roll out red fondant ⅛ inch thick and use the 1¼-inch cutter to punch out 2 circles. Utilizing the bottom of the round tips, slice off a piece of both red circles **(D)** and shape them around the bugs' bodies, gluing them on their backs. With the rolling pin, roll out black fondant ⅛ inch thick. Cut out small circles with round tip #7. Glue the spots to the bugs' backs and glue the heads onto the bodies **(E)**. Roll out red fondant thick with the rolling pin and wooden dowels. Cut out a heart with the medium cutter. Dip your fingers in shortening and round out and shape the heart, flattening out the bottom to sit it upright **(F)**. With the rolling pin, roll out white fondant ⅛ inch thick and cut out a scalloped heart with the large cutter **(G)**. Glue all pieces together and allow to dry thoroughly. Follow the flower tutorial from the circus elephant in the Step Right Up collection (p. 70) to make flowers to embellish the love bugs and heart.

SOMEWHERE OVER THE RAINBOW

Materials Needed

fondant
(black, white, red, orange, yellow, green, light blue, blue & purple)

green & gold
shimmer dust
& brushes

Cutters Needed

2¼-inch scalloped
circle cutter

round tips
#10 & #12

Tools Needed

rolling pin with ⅛-inch
& 1/16-inch guide rings

knife tool

precision knife

Sweet Tips

SIMPLIFY — Omit the rainbow and clouds and center the pot of gold. Make additional gold coins to decorate the bottom topper.

ACCENTUATE — Create additional four-leaf clovers in different sizes. Make them bigger and utilize small heart cutters or a clover cutter. Cut out additional shapes if you have any excess of your rainbow pattern.

PERSONALIZE — Cut an initial or age out of fondant and glue it to the center of the clover. Or form it from white fondant similar to the clouds.

EXPAND — Follow the tutorial to make horseshoes from the Down on the Farm collection (p. 55) and the bunny feet from the Hoppy Easter collection (p. 172) to create lucky charms.

DECORATE & DISPLAY — Place the cupcake in little black salsa bowls to resemble pots and embellish your presentation with plastic or chocolate gold coins.

Rainbow & Pot of Gold

LEVEL OF DIFFICULTY

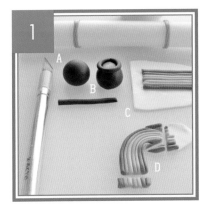

How to:

1. Roll black fondant into a ball (approximately 1 inch) **(A)** and taper the top a little. Roll out black fondant onto your work surface and wrap and glue it around the top of the pot to create the rim **(B)**. Roll out all the colors of fondant (except black and white) onto your work surface fairly thin for the rainbow colors. With the rolling pin, roll out white fondant $\frac{1}{16}$ inch thick and spread glue onto it. Layer the colorful fondant strips in order to create the rainbow **(C)**. Trim the excess white fondant with the precision knife and shape the rainbow to fit over the pot. Straighten both ends of the rainbow by cutting them, and narrow the top of the rainbow that will be sitting at the top of the pot **(D)**.

2. With the rolling pin, roll out green fondant $\frac{1}{8}$ inch thick and cut out 4 circles with round tip #12. Shape them into teardrops. With the knife tool, indent the tops to form heart shapes and then the center to form leaves **(A)**. Glue all leaves together to make a 4-leaf clover. Brush green shimmer dust onto the clover. Roll out yellow fondant $\frac{1}{8}$ inch thick and cut out several circles with round tip #10 to make gold coins. Brush gold shimmer dust onto the coins **(B)**. Glue the rainbow and coins to the pot and the clover to the end of the rainbow **(C)**. With the rolling pin, roll out white fondant $\frac{1}{8}$ inch thick. Cut out a scalloped circle with the 2¼-inch cutter for the bottom topper and various sizes of small circles with the tops and bottoms of the round tips. Roll a small circle into a ball and then roll it out on your work surface. Start at one end and roll it into itself to create a coil **(D)**. Repeat with the other circles and place and glue them onto the bottom topper to create clouds **(E)**. Glue the rainbow with the pot of gold to the topper and allow to dry thoroughly.

HOPPY EASTER

Materials Needed

fondant
*(white, pink, orange,
light green & black)*

raw spaghetti

tylose powder

Cutters Needed

1¼-inch circle cutter

round tips
#7 & #12

small circle cutter

small, medium &
large teardrop cutters

medium & large
flower cutters

Tools Needed

rolling pin with ⅛-inch
& 1/16-inch guide rings

2 wooden dowels

knife tool

modeling tool

small modeling stick

food scissors

small spatula

large ball tool

thin foam mat

Sweet Tips

SIMPLIFY	Create only the bunny bottoms rather than the entire three-dimensional bunnies. Omit the lettuce.
ACCENTUATE	Make fondant eggs by rolling fondant in different colors into balls, narrowing the tops into egg shapes.
PERSONALIZE	Follow the tutorial to make a wood sign from the Gobble 'til You Wobble collection (p. 200) to insert in the garden and write names and ages with an edible-ink marker.
EXPAND	Follow the tutorial to make carrots (minus the face) from the We Go Together like Peas & Carrots collection (p. 163) to add to the bunny garden.
DECORATE & DISPLAY	Frost and coat the tops of the cupcakes with crushed Oreo cookies for dirt and crush extra cookies to decorate your plate or cake stand. Find spring cupcake decor, such as picket fence wrappers, to enhance the presentation.

Bunny Garden

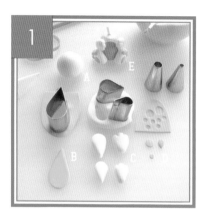

How to:

1. Knead tylose powder into white fondant and roll it into a 1-inch ball **(A)**. Shape it into an oval for the bunny's body. Carefully insert a raw spaghetti through the center by slowly twisting it in, leaving enough protruding to hold the head. With the rolling pin, roll out pink fondant 1/16 inch thick and cut out a large teardrop with the cutter **(B)**. Glue it to the front of the bunny's body, tucking the pointed side underneath. Roll out white fondant thick with the rolling pin and wooden dowels. Cut out 2 medium teardrop shapes and 2 small teardrop shapes with the respective cutters. Round out the sides of the shapes and use the knife tool to make 2 indentations on the wide end of each to form the hands and feet **(C)**. Shape the feet in front of the body slanted outward and the hands around the top. With the rolling pin, roll out pink fondant 1/16 inch thick. Cut out 2 circles with round tip #12 and shape them into teardrops. Glue them to the end of the bunny feet. Cut out an additional 6 circles with round tip #7 **(D)** and glue 3 on each foot at the toes. Glue the hands and feet to the bunny's body **(E)**.

2. Roll white fondant into a ball (approximately 2/3 inch) for the bunny's head **(A)**. Prior to drying, fit it over the raw spaghetti protruding from the body to ensure it fits. Use round tip #12 to indent a smile on the bunny's face and the small modeling stick to make whisker dots. Roll out white fondant thick with the rolling pin and wooden dowels. Cut out 2 teardrop shapes with the small cutter to form the bunny ears. Use the modeling tool to indent the center of the ears **(B)**. Roll out pink fondant with the rolling pin 1/8 inch thick and cut out 2 circles with round tip #12. Shape them into teardrops **(C)** and glue them to the center of the white ears. Use the modeling tool to indent the center again and insert 2 small raw spaghetti pieces to the bottom of the ears by slowly twisting them inside. Gently fold the two sides of the ears inward and insert them into the bunny's head. Use tools and/or cutters to prop the ears up to allow them to dry in place. Cut a circle out of the pink fondant with round tip #7 and shape it into a rounded triangle for the bunny's nose **(D)**. Glue it to the center of the bunny's face. With the rolling pin, roll out black fondant 1/8 inch thick and cut

out 2 circles with round tip #7 (E). Shape them into ovals and glue them to the bunny's face. Roll out white fondant thick with the rolling pin and wooden dowels. Punch out a small circle with the cutter. Use the food scissors make cuts around the entire circle and on its sides to shape the bunny tail (F). Glue the tail to the back of the bunny. When the ears are sufficiently dry, glue the head to the body. To make the bunny bottom, roll out white fondant thick with the rolling pin and wooden dowels. Punch out a 1¼-inch circle with the cutter. Round out the sides to form the bottom. Follow the steps above to make the bunny feet and tail and glue them onto the bottom.

3. To create the lettuce, roll light green fondant into a ball (approximately ½ inch) and set it aside to dry (A). With the rolling pin, roll out more light green fondant $\frac{1}{16}$ inch thick and cut out 3 medium and 3 large flowers with the cutters (B). Use the small spatula to make small slices where each petal connects to make them longer (C). Spread a bit of powdered sugar on the thin foam mat and place a flower on it. Pick up 1 petal with your fingers on one hand and, with the other hand, thin out the edges by slowly turning the ball tool around the petal. Do the same for all the petals, which should become ruffly (D). Repeat this step with the rest of the flower shapes. Once all flowers are ruffled, take one of the medium flowers, spread glue over the center, and insert the light green ball in the center. Fold up the petals, one at a time and repeat with the remaining medium flowers first, followed by the large flowers. Use the modeling tool to spread out any of the ruffled edges as needed (E). Allow to dry thoroughly.

SPRING CHICK

fondant
(yellow, orange & black)

round tips
#7 & #12

small teardrop cutter

rolling pin with
⅛-inch guide rings

2 wooden dowels

knife tool

Sweet Tips

SIMPLIFY	Make a two-dimensional chick lying on a flat topper.
ACCENTUATE	With the same shape as the chick's body, make eggs for extra cupcakes. Add chicks hatching out of eggs by making white eggs and attaching the feathers, feet, and facial features to the egg with some cracks.
PERSONALIZE	Make extra eggs and add fondant initials or ages to them.
EXPAND	Follow the tutorial for baby chicks from the Down on the Farm collection (p. 57) to add to your assortment.
DECORATE & DISPLAY	Make green frosting and use decorating tip #233 to pipe grass onto your cupcakes. Embellish your presentation with Easter and spring decor, such as faux grass and picket fences.

Spring Chick

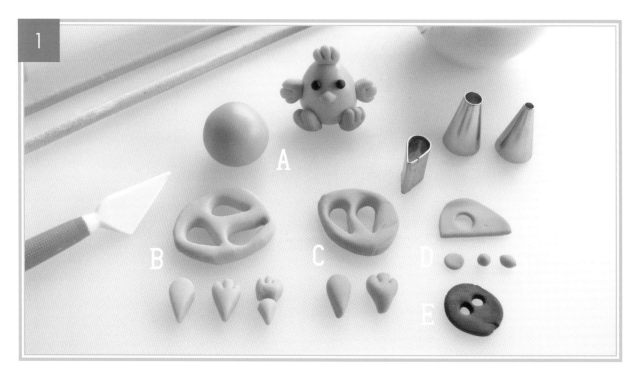

How to:

1. Roll yellow fondant into a ball (approximately 1 inch) **(A)** and shape it into an egg. Roll out more yellow fondant thick with the rolling pin and wooden dowels. Cut out 3 small teardrop shapes with the cutter. Use the knife tool to make 2 indentations on the wide end of each of the shapes. Then use the rounded edge of the teardrop cutter to trim off the bottom tips **(B)**. Glue 2 of them to the chick's side and 1 on top. Roll out orange fondant thick with the rolling pin and wooden dowels. Cut out 2 teardrop shapes with the small cutter. Make 2 indentations at the wide end with the knife tool **(C)** and shape it at the bottom of the chick to form the feet. Glue them in place. With the rolling pin, roll out more orange fondant ⅛ inch thick and use round tip #12 to cut out a circle. Roll it into a ball and then pinch the two sides to form the beak **(D)**. With the rolling pin, roll out black fondant ⅛ inch thick and cut out 2 circles with round tip #7 for the eyes **(E)**. Glue the beak and eyes to the chick. Allow to dry thoroughly.

OLÉ! CINCO DE MAYO!

Materials Needed

fondant
(yellow, red, green, orange & black)

Cutters Needed

$\frac{7}{8}$-inch & $1\frac{1}{4}$-inch circle cutters

small square cutter

medium teardrop cutter

Tools Needed

rolling pin with $\frac{1}{8}$-inch & $\frac{1}{16}$-inch guide rings

2 wooden dowels

precision knife

rolling pastry cutter

flower-forming cup

Sweet Tips

SIMPLIFY	Add only straight-lined decorations to the sombrero and maracas.
ACCENTUATE	Make additional sombreros in different colors and be creative with the embellishments.
PERSONALIZE	Use the rope technique from the Western Trails collection (p. 60) to mold them into various rope shapes, such as initials or ages.
EXPAND	Follow the tutorial to make cacti from the Western Trails collection (p. 62) for additional cupcakes. Embellish them with tiny flowers to add color.
DECORATE & DISPLAY	Coat your cupcakes with frosting and crushed graham crackers to make edible sand. Utilize Mexican-themed dishware and decorations, such as chili peppers and cacti, to enhance your presentation.

Sombrero, Maracas & Mustache

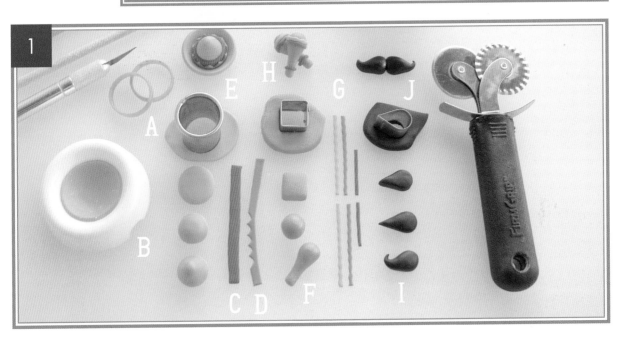

How to:

1. Roll out yellow fondant thick with the rolling pin and wooden dowels. Cut out a ⅞-inch circle with the cutter. Roll it into a ball and then shape it into a stout cone to form the top of the sombrero **(A)**. With the rolling pin, roll out yellow fondant ⅛ inch thick and cut out a 1¼-inch circle with the cutter. Sprinkle powdered sugar over the flower-forming cup and put the circle inside to dry **(B)**. With the rolling pin, roll out red fondant 1/16 inch thick and use the rolling pastry cutter to cut out a ¼-inch-wide strip **(C)**. Fit it to the bottom of the cone, trim it with the precision knife, and glue it. With the rolling pin, roll out green fondant 1/16 inch thick and use the rolling pastry cutter to cut out a thinner strip. With the corner of the small square cutter, trim the top and make a triangular pattern **(D)**. Fit it to the bottom of the cone over the red strip. Trim it with the precision knife and glue it. When the bottom of the sombrero is dry enough and holding its shape, glue the cone in the center to form the sombrero **(E)**. Roll out orange fondant thick with the rolling pin and wooden dowels. Cut out 2 small squares with the cutter. Roll them both into balls and then roll one end out with your fingers to form the maraca handles, keeping the opposite end round **(F)**. With the rolling pin, roll out yellow, green, and red fondant 1/16 inch thick. Use the fluted blade of the pastry cutter to cut very thin strips of the yellow and green fondant. Use the pastry cutter to cut straight, thin strips of the red fondant **(G)**. Fit them to the maracas, trim them with the precision knife, and glue them on, tucking them underneath. When firm enough, glue 1 maraca to the other **(H)**. Roll out black fondant thick with the rolling pin and wooden dowels. Cut out 2 medium-sized teardrops with the cutter. Round out the edges with your fingers (dipped in shortening, if necessary) and curl up the thin ends **(I)**. Join and glue the wide ends together to form the mustache **(J)**. Allow to dry thoroughly.

COULDN'T PICK A BETTER MUM

Sweet Tips

SIMPLIFY	Only make one or two flowers for each cupcake.
ACCENTUATE	Cut out the word "Mum" with letter cutters to decorate additional cupcakes.
PERSONALIZE	Follow the tutorial to make a wood sign from the Gobble 'til You Wobble collection (p. 200) to insert in the cupcake and write mom's name with an edible-ink marker.
EXPAND	Add more flowers by following the rose tutorial from the Shabby Chic Bridal Shower collection (p. 231) in matching colors.
DECORATE & DISPLAY	Present your cupcakes on floral dishes, in mason jars, or in pots. Add rustic details, such as burlap, to the packaging or presentation.

Mum Flower

LEVEL OF DIFFICULTY

How to:

1. Roll white fondant into a ball (approximately ½ inch) **(A)**. Insert raw spaghetti dipped in a bit of glue into the ball and allow it to dry thoroughly. With the rolling pin, roll out colored fondant $\frac{1}{16}$ inch thick and cut out 6–7 flowers with the large daisy cutter **(B)**. Spread a bit of powdered sugar over the thin foam mat and place a flower on it. Use the veiner tool to thin out each petal **(C)**. Repeat with the remaining flowers. Take a flower, spread glue over it, and then insert the spaghetti with the white ball through the center of the flower. Start folding up each petal over the ball until it is completely covered **(D)**. Repeat the last step for the remaining flowers. As you add each one, the petals should spread out, so make sure you don't glue the tips. When complete, place it into the flower forming up and allow it to dry thoroughly **(E)**. Repeat the process with additional colors. (For small flowers, start with a smaller ball and use the small daisy cutter.)

DAPPER DAD

Materials Needed

fondant
(brown, teal, maroon & white)

Cutters Needed

1¼-inch, 1½-inch,
2¼-inch & 2½-inch
circle cutters

round tip #7

large square cutter

Tools Needed

rolling pin with
⅛-inch guide rings

4 wooden dowels

precision knife

small modeling stick

rolling pastry cutter

square embossing mat

Sweet Tips

SIMPLIFY	Omit the top hat from the topper.
ACCENTUATE	Make more top hats for additional cupcakes.
PERSONALIZE	Cut out the word "Dad" with letter cutters to decorate additional cupcakes.
EXPAND	Follow the tutorial to create an argyle pattern from the Fore collection (p. 137) for the vest or on additional toppers.
DECORATE & DISPLAY	Gift or present your cupcakes in leather or kraft boxes to make the presentation more masculine.

Top Hat, Vest & Bow Tie

How to:

1. Roll out brown fondant thick with the rolling pin and wooden dowels. Cut out a 1½-inch circle with the cutter. Roll it into a ball and shape it into a cylinder. Narrow the cylinder at the bottom and flatten out the top. Use your fingers to slightly pinch the perimeter of the top of the hat (**A**). With the rolling pin, roll out more brown fondant ⅛ inch thick and cut out a 1¼-inch circle with the cutter. Place it between 2 wooden dowels, fold the sides up, and tighten the width of the dowels to hold them in place. Place the top hat in the center to measure properly (**B**). With the rolling pin, roll out more brown fondant ⅛ inch thick and use the rolling pastry cutter to cut a strip (**C**). Form it around the base of the top hat, trim it, and glue it to the bottom. Glue the top hat to the center of the brim and allow to dry thoroughly.

2. With the rolling pin, roll out teal fondant ⅛ inch thick and spread a bit of shortening over the fondant. Place the square embossing mat over the fondant and use the rolling pin to impress the pattern onto it. Use the 2½-inch cutter to punch out a circle (**A**). Use the large square cutter to cut a triangle out of the top and then a smaller one out of the bottom. Use the 1½-inch circle cutter to trim the sides for the sweater vest arm holes (**B**). With the rolling pin, roll out white fondant ⅛ inch thick and cut out a 2¼-inch circle with the cutter. Glue the teal sweater shape onto the white topper and use the 2¼-inch cutter to trim it to size (**C**). Use a side of the large square cutter to indent the center of the sweater vest. With the rolling pin, roll out maroon fondant ⅛ inch thick and cut out a strip with the rolling pastry cutter. Turn it upside down and fold over both sides to meet in the middle. Glue them and pinch the middle together to form the bow (**D**). Cut out a smaller strip of the maroon fondant (**E**), fit it over the center of the bow, and glue it down. Use the precision knife to make 2 indentations where the bow meets the center on each side and glue it to the vest. With the maroon fondant, cut out 3 circles with round tip #7 and glue them to the vest as buttons. Use the small modeling stick to make 2 indentations in each button for button holes. Allow to dry thoroughly.

RED, WHITE & BOOM

Materials Needed

fondant
(red, white & blue)

white & blue
shimmer dust
& brushes

lollipop sticks

raw spaghetti

Cutters Needed

round tip #12

miniature, small,
medium & large
star cutters

small circle cutter

large daisy
flower cutter

"4" number cutter

Tools Needed

rolling pin with
⅛-inch guide rings

2 wooden dowels

precision knife

small modeling stick

Sweet Tips

SIMPLIFY	Omit the firework from the fourth star or don't pull the flower petals apart.
ACCENTUATE	Make many different colors and sizes of fireworks on sticks. Punch out "USA" with letter cutters.
PERSONALIZE	Add initials or age in lieu of the "4" on the star.
EXPAND	Follow the confetti tutorial from the Piece of Cake collection (p. 21). Create word bubbles based on the tutorial from the To the Rescue collection (p. 91), replacing the letters with "USA."
DECORATE & DISPLAY	Embellish with patriotic cupcake liners and wrappers.

Fireworks

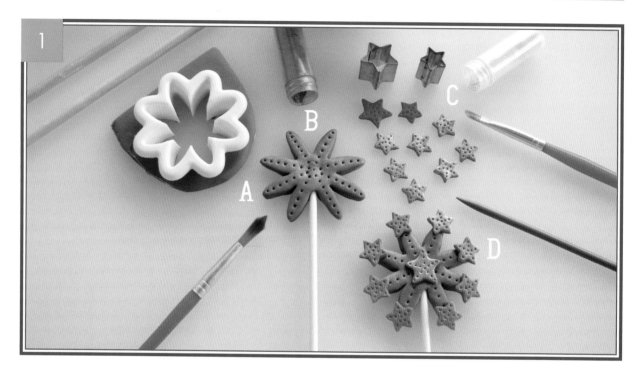

How to:

1. Roll blue fondant thick with the rolling pin and wooden dowels. Cut out a flower with the large daisy cutter **(A)**. Gently pull the ends of the petals to elongate them. Insert a lollipop stick between 2 petals by gently turning while pushing upward. Use the small modeling stick to indent dots from the center out toward the ends of the petals. Brush it with blue shimmer dust **(B)**. With the rolling pin, roll out red fondant ⅛ inch thick. Cut out 1 small star and 8 miniature stars with the cutters. Indent dots from the center toward the ends of the stars' points and brush white shimmer dust on them **(C)**. Glue the medium star in the center of the blue flower and the remaining miniature stars at the ends of the flower petals to create the firework **(D)**. Repeat the process with different colors to form additional fireworks.

Fourth Star

LEVEL OF DIFFICULTY

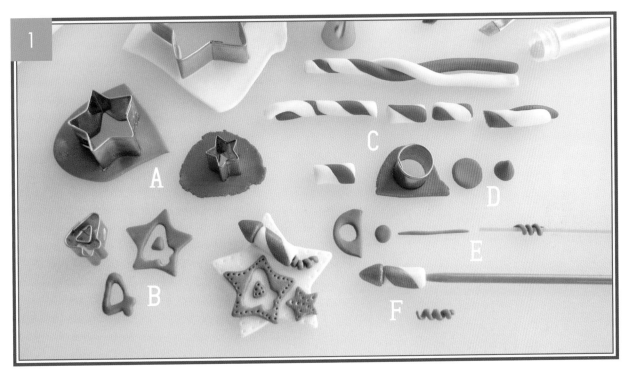

How to:

1. With the rolling pin, roll out white, blue, and red fondant ⅛ inch thick. Cut a large star out of the white, a medium star out of the blue, and a small star out of the red with the respective cutters **(A)**. Use the small modeling stick to indent small dots around the perimeter of the white and blue stars and from the center to the points of the red star. Cut a "4" out of the blue star, but discard the actual "4" and keep the silhouette in the star, along with the piece in the center of the number **(B)**. Take red and white fondant and roll them onto your work surface to form equally sized strips. Hold the ends of both colors together and begin twisting the colors together; then roll it onto your work surface to adhere both the white and red fondant together. Use the precision knife to cut into small cylinders to create the firework tubes **(C)**. With the rolling pin, roll red fondant ⅛ inch thick and cut a small circle with the cutter. Roll it into a ball and shape it into a cone **(D)**. With the rolling pin, roll out blue fondant ⅛ inch thick and cut a circle with round tip #12. Roll it into a ball and then roll it all the way out onto your work surface. Coil it around a piece of raw spaghetti to dry a bit **(E)**. Glue the red cone to the red-and-white cylinder and use the small modeling stick to make a hole at the bottom. Then insert and glue the blue coil into the bottom of the firework and glue the firework to the top of the large white star **(F)**. Glue on the blue "4" star and small red star. Allow to dry thoroughly.